Read What Others Can't:
Master Your Social and Communication Skills

Read What Others Can't

Master Your Social and Communication Skills

I J Nayak

India
2023

CONTENTS

It would be wonderful if humans could understand what happens inside our brains--one of the most complex organs ever devised--where great ideas and innovations take shape. Couldn't it be wonderful if even scientists and technology could unlock its mysteries--an integral component that has no equivalent replacement in machines today?

So what goes on inside our brains?

One could argue that knowing what people actually think would help improve communications and protect us from potential danger. Reading people may sound impossible but may prove crucial in eliminating second-guessing or making incorrect judgments in everyday situations with coworkers, strangers and loved ones alike.

What does it take to accurately interpret people? Ideally, fancy degrees would provide sufficient knowledge of its inner workings; otherwise it may depend on intuitive powers inherited from parents or hidden secrets one needs to unlock - I believe that all factors play a part.

Even with all of the books ever written about brain function, reading people accurately remains impossible. Good genes or any top secrets revealed via Google search won't help either; to truly comprehend someone's inner workings requires science - understanding why people think what they do and react how they do are the keys to understanding another individual.

Deciphering carefully guarded secrets requires knowledge, observation and comprehension of events as well as strong intuitive powers to reach accurate conclusions. Most importantly, however, is finding the appropriate direction and starting the journey!

And this book encapsulates that purpose. It breaks down science into manageable pieces to give readers all of the information needed to read minds in an easy and interesting manner. Through all my years teaching people effective communication techniques, I've come to recognize that information that doesn't directly benefit one's purpose can quickly become useless - while knowing about what happens to the left side of your brain when drawing a bird with right hand can be fascinating, it becomes pointless if not planned on drawing with it in future.

Therefore, I have carefully selected scientific information that is tailored specifically for your purpose of reading other people's minds. I avoided complex terminology and stuck to what's essential: simple findings with clear explanations.

But that is only one aspect of mind reading; there's so much more. There are the secrets, self-evaluations, subtle signs and communication tricks one can employ in order to become a more attuned listener. I use the analogy of the rising sun when teaching students about mastering any craft.

I ask my students what time the sun rises each morning. Those who wake up early have some idea when the sun comes up, compared to those who sleep late; none can give an exact minute as no one has been motivated enough or observant enough to know exactly when. So then, I give them an exercise - something which I encourage you to also do yourself now.

Imagine sitting on your balcony every morning before the sun rises and reading a newspaper while sipping coffee - would it be easy for you to know exactly when the sun came up? Your answer might be more accurate since being there when it happened gives a good understanding of its "window of time".

Imagine sitting on a balcony facing east, gazing upon the exact location where the sun rises, watching as its warmth tinted the sky with golden hues on the horizon and then checking your watch immediately; your accuracy would be unrivaled on that particular day because you had knowledge of where it rises from and were focused on your task at hand; your intuition would also kick in, enabling accurate estimates even without direct observation - you would know exactly when the sun would rise despite constantly shifting time zones!

Now if I were to ask a classroom of students what time the sun rises, those that had truly committed themselves to discovering it would provide the most accurate response. That is exactly how mind reading works; it requires knowledge, observation and an appreciation that every individual thinks differently so there is no "one size fits all" solution that applies.

Understanding all of the factors involved when observing someone requires knowledge and commitment. You need a solid strategy for steering you in the right direction - that's where this book comes in - I provide you with everything you need to become an adept reader.

This book disproves myths and unreliable information available online about reading people. For example, having arms folded may signal defensiveness; but in a cold room or sitting on an armless chair this behavior could simply be due to environmental influences rather than personality traits.

Believing or reading random, unsubstantiated "facts" is both unnecessary and harmful; misreading people is worse than not knowing them at all! Mind reading doesn't involve spying or intrusiveness - rather it involves understanding what someone's really meaning when speaking or communicating to us; understanding their thoughts enables us to become aware of their emotions when responding.

Fact is, only 7% of communication takes place verbally - the rest takes place non-verbally. Mind reading involves understanding what someone else is experiencing by knowing their true intentions behind what they're saying versus what has gone unsaid - something this highly informative and well-researched book provides more than just as theoretical approach to mind reading.

This book offers targeted knowledge and understanding, anecdotes from my own experiences and learning, and a complete comprehensive approach that leaves no stone unturned when it comes to understanding the unsaid world. We'll also examine different personality types, motivations and objectives so you can get an understanding of exactly how certain individuals think, why they communicate the way they do and how you can achieve personal goals through their messages - so lets get going now.

What is Mind Reading? At first glance, mind reading might appear to be some form of sorcery or unethical practice to pry into people's private thoughts and wreak havoc upon them; knowing someone could read your mind would likely cause alarm, regardless of your relationship status with them; knowing they had such power could make us flee in terror - there could never be greater superpower than knowing everything happening inside our brains! But in reality it is more about understanding than invasion.

Mind reading is about creating confidence when talking to someone, knowing their message won't get misrepresented or misunderstood. Mind reading enables us to comprehend unsaid words and strengthen communications between parties involved - an invaluable skill that will allow you to build stronger connections both professionally and personally.

Our favorite people tend to be those who listen closely and understand us; people like the pediatrician or dentist who knew when our "I'm fine" didn't sound quite right; strangers on buses who understood when we changed bodyweight, giving up seats when necessary.

These people listen, observe and comprehend our needs and emotions with compassion and understanding; they're not intrusive but instead provide invaluable support. Their powers include knowing exactly what needs to be done as well as having the skills needed to build long-term relationships through this almost superhuman ability - exactly the type of people we secretly wish we were more like - not born with this ability but having made a conscious decision to be more aware of others around them.

Mind readers knew how important effective communication was; they understood that effective dialogue required deep listening and an in-depth comprehension of what was said beyond words. They paid equal attention to silence, tone, motivation, intentions of speakers as well as being aware of their environments and people while looking beyond prejudices, judgements and limitations to assess conversations in order to deduce hidden truths - in return gaining trust, understanding respect as well as making better judgements and decisions both professionally and personally.

Mind reading is like having someone translate a foreign language for you. They could do it literally or explain their motivation behind certain foreign-sounding words that were said.

People reading isn't just another craft or trick used to invade someone's privacy; rather it's an art that pays respect to an individual's emotions and thoughts.

Learning how to read people is one of the best ways to ensure conversations flow smoothly and take place at full circle. Mind-reading skills will take away any guesswork during conversations and replace it with understanding, compassion and relationship building elements. Mind reading abilities can greatly alter interactions at networking events, workplace meetings or when meeting someone you find highly attractive;

mind-reading abilities could have an incredible effect on outcomes of interactions between two individuals.

Mind reading is an art that requires in-depth knowledge about how the human brain operates, being present mentally, avoiding judgments and making observations - but most importantly it involves creating the ideal combination of all these requirements to understand someone else's thoughts regardless of who they are, their personality or your relationship status with them.

Mind reading is an in-depth topic, so we will cover each facet individually before providing strategies on how to apply these insights to create the perfect environment for mind reading!

Part One covers everything you'll need in order to embark on this journey of understanding people and communication. It outlines what can be expected when trying to read people and the mistakes or obstructions we may encounter when trying to interpret what someone else is communicating; furthermore it addresses some of the challenges we encounter today in an ever-evolving communications arena.

Part Two explores everything related to our minds. It outlines how our brain works and identifies individual differences as genetic. Furthermore, this part will help you gain an insight into why people behave in certain ways and explores various personality types - so that you can view people more objectively and make better judgments of them.

Part Three focuses on you and what you bring to the table. There are two major aspects to understanding someone: knowing their way of thinking and understanding YOURS. Unfortunately, mental barriers often impede us in properly comprehending someone. Our own tendency to quickly judge and draw assumptions based on personal biases prevent us from understanding others correctly.

Part Four entails taking everything that has been learned thus far and applying these principles into practice. Here you'll discover little secrets and strategies on how you can infer the true meaning behind words, spot deceits, and gain full mastery over someone else's mind.

Needless to say, you are embarking upon a complete book and comprehensive resource on becoming an investigation officer-grade people reader.

Part One: Lay the Foundation

Beginning any new journey requires understanding its motivations for action taken and why certain behaviors occur. You need to know why mind reading is necessary and anticipate any challenges through its process; why does what's being expressed not translate directly?

Not so long ago, communication involved sitting face to face with another person with eyes locked together and having ample time for both of you to speak and be heard. Over time however, communication methods have changed considerably - while new forms have allowed for global interactions, they also reduce quality interactions due to multitasking taking place simultaneously with conversation taking place between you. This means conversations have lost their value.

Lack of Time

Our time is constantly on the line. Although today's technologies offer us some relief - pre-cooked meals may reduce mealtime to mere seconds per meal and virtual meetings often schedule meetings in transit to save time - coffees have become on-the-go and communications often timed around mental check lists that we create in our minds.

Gone Are the Days of Distant Communication That Limit Interaction

Long gone are the days when we either communicated in-person or wrote lengthy letters that could take months to send; when each word counted for something in its final draft. Nowadays, communication takes many different forms - which often limits interaction.

Today there are numerous means of communicating with another individual: emails, text messages, social media interactions, voice notes, video calls and phone calls are just a few methods available to us for communication. Meeting someone face to face has mostly been replaced with Zoom meetings or video calls as discussed topics have moved online - the major downside being these forms of digital conversation limit the overall dialogue experience.

Text messages don't allow us to accurately gauge someone's tone and facial expressions, so responding with one-word answers could be due to boredom, disagreement or being distracted from communicating with multiple other parties simultaneously.

An interview conducted over the phone limits your ability to understand how a recruiter is receiving and processing your answers. Since there's no interaction between yourself and them, accurately understanding others can become increasingly challenging.

Social Media Conversationalists

Anonymity can be an incredible power; it enables you to become invisibly dominant while giving you the ability to have your voice heard without accountability; giving others access to untold riches without restriction from passport controls is like having wings without limitations on where or when you fly.

Only limited by typing speed, typing anonymity makes you say things you might otherwise never say directly to someone in person.

Random thoughts become opinions, which then turn into debates. You never know whether the person criticizing your hairstyle truly dislikes it or they just had a bad hair day themselves; their freedom of speech makes it impossible to grasp how people think and perceive specific information.

Global Communications across Cultures

No longer do we communicate solely within our local communities, now that businesses and relationships span borders. Cultures have become intermixed as our modes of interaction have spread worldwide - what was considered respectful behavior at one end may now be seen as offensive in another corner. Embarkation will take time as we adapt and accept these differences with each other while learning how to coexist and communicate more efficiently across borders.

Not only must we overcome language barriers, but often, it may be necessary to accept that another person's indifference to eye contact might not be due to boredom but rather respect. Over time we must develop a mutually acceptable way of communicating between cultures.

As these global communications become ever more impactful, their effects are felt most keenly at home; often resulting in confusion and shock rather than the inability of people to understand others.

Long ago, conversations centered around hunting, family, children and survival. Though conversations centered on these subjects, now there's so much more we can discuss - from banking and investments to sports, technology and even digitalization, there are so many topics and subtopics which could be discussed at length.

Interests have never been so diverse; maintaining conversations across them can be an extremely difficult challenge. Your mind can wander easily when talking with someone whose interests diverge significantly from yours; this leads to confusion and misinterpretations of actions, making reading someone's mind even harder than before.

As our world rapidly changes, it can be challenging to keep pace with its rapid advancement and hold meaningful and productive conversations with people. In order to do this successfully and read them accurately, it is necessary to remain mindful of these factors while evolving at an equal pace.

What Does it Take to Land an Amazing Job? mes If it were simply up to schooling and college grades alone, in-person interviews wouldn't even be necessary. Have you ever received an offer after simply browsing LinkedIn profiles of potential job candidates and being impressed by current work positions? That is highly unlikely; degrees don't always indicate whether someone makes an ideal candidate.

Businesses care deeply about your mindset, habits, and how well your thoughts and values align with those of the company - an aspect which carries over into life as well. For instance, when choosing a life partner it's not simply about looking for comedians; rather you should find someone with whom you share similar understanding of how the world works through nonverbal means such as touching hands.

It is true that life and people can often be complex; no one comes with an easy answer when it comes to communication or social relationships. No warning sign alerting us of lies, abuse or bullying behaviors can always be found visible on their surface. Studies of human nature have led to many remarkable revelations. There are patterns in verbal and physical behavior which reveal these truths with remarkable accuracy, often studied closely by professionals dedicated to understanding this aspect of our existence. Individuals in such roles include secret agents, psychologists, investigators, counselors and jurors. Their study of human patterns allows them to quickly determine if someone is being honest, concealing secrets or engaging in criminal behavior - thus helping them make sounder judgments to safeguard both themselves and others from potential danger.

Needless to say, interpersonal communication skills are largely neglected in society today. Therefore, they should be taught at schools and colleges regardless of the program students select; people reading shouldn't just be limited to psychological studies either; marketers, doctors, nurses, lawyers, recruiters, sportspeople - any professional that deals with people should also learn this skill.

Mastery in Communications and People Reading
People reading is an under-valued skill that often goes unappreciated, just like its relation to speaking. Not everyone thinks in the same way and speaks in the same manner - all depending on upbringing, environment, emotions and personality types that affect what we say - meaning one person may say one thing but another could interpret it completely differently; ultimately it boils down to being able to read people accurately enough in order to accurately deduce what each other person means by what they are trying to say

Relationships According to Henry Winkler, assumptions are the termites of relationships - an observation which couldn't be more true! No matter who it involves; spouse, parents, friends or siblings: assumptions and misunderstandings often serve as the main catalysts in creating conflict in these relationships; often misinterpreted as lack of interest on their part or an attempt by one sibling or another to share an achievement being considered rubbing it in. There are numerous times throughout our daily lives when something we say could be taken out of context entirely or misinterpreted completely differently by others - making us question their intentions!

If only they understood what we truly meant, emotions or heartfelt grievances wouldn't be misconstrued as detachments and complaints. Too often we expect close relations to pick up on subtle hints, moods, veiled messages, or innuendo without us needing to state ourselves directly; isn't that why communicating is such an artform: to understand what others mean without having to speak up yourself?

At times it can be challenging to accurately read signs in relationships. Understanding, concentration and an aware mind are all required if we want to accurately interpret those signs; once acquired it can make a tremendous difference in maintaining healthy relationships. We had one couple living next door that believed her husband twitched every time he lied to her; as a result of which they frequently got into fights!

Every time she would ask him a tricky question, we would all carefully observe his upper lip covered by an impressive mustache and watch as it began twitching in response. My impression at that time was: She knew exactly how to spot when he was lying! This information didn't bode well as they often fought over it - until years later when they sought therapy where they learned it twitched not because he was lying but rather due to nervousness! Such assumptions caused so much harm in their relationship!

Accurately reading people could help you overcome such assumptions, enabling you to better comprehend relationships despite how well someone may express themselves verbally.

Career

Had you known that your boss wasn't experiencing problems outside the work place that were delaying the completion of his work on time, rather than simply being frustrated about having it delivered late, your approach may have been different: offering moral support and space instead of constantly criticising delays would likely yield stronger emotional bonds with him or her and can open doors to opportunities, improved relations and more effective teamwork.

Most jobs involve working together in teams in order to produce results, whether as doctors, teachers or managers. No matter your specialty - from medicine and teaching through management roles - understanding and working well with other professionals is crucial in accomplishing work efficiently and to your best ability. Leaders in particular must collaborate with a wide variety of individuals - each possessing different talents, shortcomings and reactions when faced with challenges or criticism - by understanding why someone responds as they do, you can tailor responses appropriately and make optimal use of their abilities.

Companies today are investing heavily in creating an enjoyable working environment for their employees, realizing that employees are their greatest investment and should remain contented and happy in order to perform at their maximum capacity. Incentives are increasingly offered with greater emphasis placed on employee satisfaction. Companies must respect each employee's individuality while meeting emotional needs accordingly; reading can provide businesses with an effective tool to achieve this. People reading can also help employees retain employees by creating an atmosphere conducive to wellbeing and productivity.

Social Life
People are essential to our wellbeing; they support emotional wellbeing, basic needs and overall mental well-being. All humans desire being heard and understood, so people who provide safe spaces for others to do just that often attract the right energies - imagine speaking to someone who understood exactly what you were trying to say without needing endless explanations; you would likely seek that person out at every event possible!

Mental and Emotional Health Understanding our own thoughts can be challenging enough; often times our reactions stem from unrelated sources - lack of sleep can make you cranky or tipsy, while small things could easily set off our reactions without us realizing why they did. Emotional intelligence plays a huge part in maintaining both our emotional and mental wellbeing, by helping us recognize and comprehend our own emotions; reading aloud adds another level of insight as it lets us decipher other people's intentions more readily, such as understanding that an outburst from your partner could just as easily come from being two years old who has missed their napping session!
Understanding people can help you remain calm and positive even in times of high emotions. By distancing yourself from taunts or fits that may seem directed toward you but are actually caused by others, understanding will allow you to remain positive even during times of turmoil and difficulty.
Reading people may take time and practice, but mastering it is worth your while in creating stronger relationships both with other people and yourself. At work it will enable more productive teamwork while in your social life it can create stronger networks of friends by offering them a safe space to understand and communicate freely.

What prevents us from understanding people? Although word-for-word mind reading remains out of the realm of possibility for now, no amount of artificial intelligence, technological, or medical advances has managed to decode the complex neural circuitry within us all - yet something still stops us from accurately comprehending spoken language?

What Are You Blocking You From Reading People Correctly?

Are You Struggling with Understanding People Properly? So what's stopping you from correctly deciphering what people mean with certain actions and words? Reading people should be as straightforward as understanding facial expressions, tone, and dialogue from others, yet this doesn't always happen - same words spoken by same individuals at various occasions can mean entirely different meanings!

Someone may say to you "I know what you mean," yet their tone could indicate either complimenting or criticizing.

At times, it can be easy to pick up on someone's tone; other times it may not. We could misinterpret what someone means due to any number of reasons; here are a few factors that impact how we interpret people:

Knowing them too well or not well enough: As your relationship strengthens with someone, their expectations of you increase accordingly. Our loved ones expect us to understand what they mean without needing to explain themselves or communicate effectively. "Eyes should speak," when you know someone intimately, but they often miscommunicate when not in the right mindset. There's always more behind every look than meets the eye; sometimes that story might even remain unknown to you! What someone says or means can vary widely depending on their personality, environment, thoughts and other daily influences - it can be hard to know exactly why someone might be in an unhappy mood; could be because their boss gave them grief.

Similar to misinterpreting words and actions of someone we don't know well enough, not knowing someone enough can also lead to misinterpretations of words and actions. An introvert doesn't have anything against you - they simply take longer opening up than most. Therefore, trying to read everyone on an equal level will likely end in failure.

Overlooking Context and Focusing on Signs: Avoiding eye contact could indicate someone is lying; but it could also signal disinterest or low self-esteem; one of the worst mistakes one could make when trying to read people is applying what one reads without considering context and taking all aspects into consideration when trying to read someone. When reading people you must take into account all factors rather than solely using pieces of information from one book as evidence against one person.

Falling for the Poker Face: Don't make assumptions solely based on body language, words, or facial expressions when reading people. Reading people involves collecting data on individuals before carefully analyzing it to form accurate guesses about them. For instance, don't assume someone is nervous just because their palms are sweaty - look out for other signs too that indicate similar nervousness like fidgeting, looking nervous when speaking out loud, stuttering when speaking etc... It could just be that they are wearing too many layers and feeling too hot inside!

Unaware of Your Emotions: It could just be that you are so consumed with how someone else is behaving that you fail to assess how you feel based on how the other person acts or your own perception of them? Perhaps your own biases, prejudices or understanding of them is keeping you from seeing the big picture; in order to accurately read people it starts with self-awareness and an understanding of how you perceive people.

Mistaking Personality or Situation desfasoealing Behavior There are two key components that influence someone's actions--their environment and personality traits. Unfortunately, it can be challenging to differentiate between the two when communicating with strangers and acquaintances, leading to incorrect assessments of what people are trying to communicate. Jumping too quickly to conclusions means giving yourself enough time to understand if how someone responds is due to personal preferences or external forces that they must contend with.

Give into Confirmation Bias: When we form preconceived notions about someone and associate labels with them in our mind, anything they say or do thereafter serves to substantiate these assessments of them and confirm our own thoughts about them. By doing this, however, we can prevent ourselves from seeing the full picture and focus instead on what we perceive to be reality.

Giving in to Personality Bias: When we find someone attractive, our minds create an overly positive image of them in our minds. This also applies to people whose habits, hobbies, or choices resemble ours; our opinions tend to be more favorable of someone we feel drawn towards compared to someone different than we expected - thus hindering accurate assessments about who that person truly is.

Influence from your past: If someone recently deceived you, chances are, you might be more reluctant to trust what someone says now. Our past experiences can shape how we judge other people.

Inflexibility: If you hold strong opinions about something and someone disagrees with them, mental barriers may form to keep from accepting and understanding each other fully and objectively. For instance, if you prefer spending your money wisely and are dedicated to smart investing strategies, this might lead to you negatively judging those who spend without regard for these matters.

Fact is, we all have preconceived notions about what is considered acceptable behavior from other people. While it's perfectly fine to gravitate toward or mix with those with similar ideologies and thought processes, harboring strong judgments of people that don't fit our ideologies can create barriers between understanding how others think and behave and us fully comprehending their viewpoints and behaviors. In order to truly comprehend others and accept their differences.

Environment, upbringing and personality all play a role in how we communicate; our environment, upbringing and personality traits all influence our words, thoughts and actions. Personality experts have identified specific traits and methods of communication people typically utilize: Personlichkeit Assertive; Aggressive; Passive-Aggressive

* Manipulative

As you become better acquainted with people, your ability to identify their communication style becomes greater. Understanding why someone speaks a certain way will also increase. At first glance, passive communicators tend to avoid eye contact and agree with everything that you say, so being able to recognize their communication style will allow for more accurate assessments of personality traits and relationships. Specific situations and relationships require different forms of dialogue. Communication styles differ based on who is speaking; you may use passive-aggressive strategies when dealing with people you dislike and more manipulative methods when speaking to strangers. Understanding these styles will benefit not only yourself, but others as well. So let's dive deeper to see how each communication style works and identify similar styles in other people.

Assertive Communication Style

This communication style is widely considered one of the most effective forms. Someone using this approach has firm convictions and doesn't shy away from sharing them; they speak clearly without belittling someone else's beliefs; respect different viewpoints while freely expressing their own; they exhibit high self-esteem while seeking consensus and compromise during discussions.

Assertive communicators can easily be identified by the fact they often use "I" when speaking. For instance, they might say things such as, "I believe we need to be more supportive of her views" instead of phrase it as: "You should be more accommodating of all viewpoints". These individuals also tend to exhibit positive attitudes when communicating.

Below are a few telltale signs of someone with an assertive communication style: * They confidently express their needs and desires.

* They maintain eye contact. * They do not hesitate in saying no when appropriate. * They allow everyone an equal chance to contribute their ideas.

* They use "I" statements.

To communicate effectively with an assertive speaker, allow them to express their thoughts freely and allow them to articulate exactly how they feel when given the space to do so. Assertive people tend to share their viewpoints freely when given this chance, making them easier than other styles to read and interpret if you find something confusing; just ask your queries! They'll happily provide all the answers!

Aggressive Communication Style

People using this communication style tend to be aggressive and hostile. Their goal in conversations is always to win at all costs and they often believe their contribution to conversations is far greater than other participants' contributions. Content and context both tend to get lost due to how these people deliver their messages - with aggressive communicators often employing intimidating and belittling tone when speaking; such individuals may push back harder against those with similar styles, making their interactions quite challenging to read due to all they say being lost in their struggle for dominance of conversations.

Below are a few telltale signs that someone has an aggressive communication style: * They tend to talk over others. * They frequently point fingers. * And lastly they frown.

* These people tend to intimidate, belittle, criticize and threaten others. Its They are also demanding and controlling.

* Communicators who express their ideas or thoughts with an aggressive tone tend to use statements like "because I said so!" to assert their authority. The major distinction between an assertive and aggressive communicator is their desire for dominance; an assertive communicator prefers leading rather than being directed. When speaking with someone with an aggressive style, try keeping conversations focused and on-topic; even if conversations veer off, bring them back by making assessments about what they are saying rather than taking their tone into consideration when trying to understand their message.

Passive Communication Style

Also referred to as submissive communication style, passive communicators tend to focus on pleasing other people by avoiding conflicts and keeping conversations going in an amicable manner. They dislike confrontation and frequently respond by agreeing or saying yes. Contrary to what may appear initially, people with this communication style don't always engage in positive dialogue - their ineffective ability to convey their viewpoints can lead to much resentment and negativity over time; passive communicators find it challenging expressing themselves clearly while passive communicators's can even make them difficult read since we hardly hear their thoughts expressing themselves openly!

Here are some signs that an individual is engaging in passive communication:

* They rarely make eye contact.

* Their posture is subpar. * Their attitude tends to be one of "go with the flow".

* People with this style often have difficulty saying no. In order to effectively communicate with people of this style, it's best to ask many questions and encourage them to express their viewpoints.

Passive-Aggressive Communication Style

Everyone has their own shade of grey in communication; the Passive-Aggressive Communication Style is no exception. An amalgamation of two different approaches to communications, it encompasses passive behavior upfront with aggression waiting in the wings at any sign of conflict; these individuals may appear pleasant but may harbor considerable resentments and anger beneath the surface.

Resentment often manifests itself in gossip, sarcasm, patronizing behavior or indirect comments and remarks that express frustrations indirectly. People with this communication style typically are dealing with unresolved problems and demonstrate them indirectly by using passive-aggressive communication styles: * They use sarcasm frequently * Their words do not align with their actions * They struggle to acknowledge emotions

* Their facial expressions don't match what they're saying.

They may use phrases such as, "Don't get upset! It was just a joke!" or, "No matter what happens; I don't care!" and can often come off as passive aggressive or mean when communicating their intentions; thus making this the hardest to interpret since most of what they say comes from unresolved conflicts and issues.

People using the Manipulative Communication Style People employing this communication style rely on deceit and influence to shape the outcome of conversations and other people's actions with words. Their speech can often be difficult to decode because every word they utter seems motivated by what they're hoping to gain; their true intentions often remain hidden beneath layers of deception or manipulations; these people can often appear patronizing and will try their hardest until you agree with what they say.

Following are a few signs you are speaking with someone with a manipulative style: * They typically make statements with great conviction. * They tend not to respond well when confronted by conflicting points of view. * They hold your gaze for longer.

* They utilize hand gestures when speaking.

When engaging in dialogue with these speakers, patience and calm should be demonstrated in equal measures. Try not to react emotionally by remaining assertive but firm in your convictions; do not allow their views to sway your own opinions but don't disagree either or they will isolate themselves. Communicative styles reveal much about an individual; of course they depend on who one is communicating with; by paying close attention to these styles you can tailor responses appropriately and gain greater insight into understanding people more thoroughly

Culture is the result of many different elements coming together: traditions, folklore, rituals, language use, lifestyle choices and beliefs - these all contribute to shaping how we communicate and understand each other. Culture doesn't just exist geographically - two people in a relationship develop their own distinct culture over time as their communication, language usage and rituals influence and shape it further - just like different businesses, regions or all sorts of relationships do too!

When trying to understand someone, you must also gain an understanding of their culture. Knowing where someone hails from; their beliefs and habits; as well as any individual rituals or customs which make them special is crucial in developing empathy for that individual.

People accustomed to following certain rules and customs tend to interact differently from those with diverse rituals. Someone used to attending meetings where no one arrives on time won't appreciate its importance as much, leading them into believing their lack of time management skills are due to discipline issues rather than cultural adaptation.

An individual hailing from a culture characterized by certain styles, languages and forms of communication will likely bring these influences with them when communicating with someone from outside their own culture.

As an observer trying to read people, you should pay close attention to their cultural background. Keep in mind that this includes not only their religion and ethnicity, but also any additional small cultures that may have developed due to belonging to specific communities, organizations or other influences.

Communications and cultures are interdependent. Culture emerges through interactions among individuals that foster mutual communication to produce patterns, laws, rules and rituals that shape society as a whole. Our communications form the backbone of culture which constantly evolves through global communications that have become a daily necessity.

People of various cultures and ethnicities frequently interact through different modes.

Culture today has come to encompass much more than simply one way of being and doing things; depending on who a community or society interacts with socially or professionally there may be various cultures and rituals within that space.

As such, reading and understanding people is becoming both easier and more challenging in equal measures. To better comprehend one another we must break down assumptions and create spaces which provide space for varying beliefs, rules, and rituals under the same roof. However there can be specific challenges faced when communicating and understanding people from various cultures such as:

People communicate differently. Our languages vary as do the words and phrases we use. Even phrases as seemingly straightforward as "whatever you want" could have different interpretations across cultures; thumbs-up can either be positive or offensive depending on who it was given to. From seating arrangements to distance differences between individuals, everything is understood differently across nations around the globe.

Not everyone handles conflict the same way; some might view it as a means to reach productive conclusions while others see it as being challenged. When communicating across cultures, you must be sensitive to other people's feelings and pay close attention to how they react to specific actions taken by you or other parties involved.

Respect personal space. Covid-19 may have forced us to develop social distance, but other cultures don't accept physical contact and close proximity either. When trying to read people accurately, be wary of these specifics and try not to transgress upon anyone's personal space by moving too close or forcing yourself in too early.

As people living in this vastly varied world, we depend on one another for survival and fulfillment. To meet this need effectively, it is vital that we are considerate of one another's cultural differences and limitations. You cannot expect to accurately read someone without first understanding what has shaped their words and actions; what someone says could be reflective of all their life beliefs and experiences - showing kindness can go a long way in strengthening bonds between us all.

After engaging in conversation with a friend, you suddenly realize they've stopped responding significantly and just nod along to whatever you say without providing much input of their own. At that moment, you wish you knew how to read their mood accurately - something which takes patience and understanding; yet surely achievable!

Reading people can transform how you approach them and vice versa. Understanding people's emotions and needs allows you to respond in the appropriate manner and deepen relationships. Adjusting communication styles and tones to connect more deeply with people. However, what should you focus on when trying to read people? Understanding why they act the way they do can provide insight into human psychology; that's exactly what this section will cover!

Part Two focuses on understanding the human mind through centuries of research, scientific findings, and an examination of human nature. We cover different theories that help uncover different personality types and basic human needs that motivate people's thought patterns and behaviors - knowledge which will prove invaluable when dealing with different people from all walks of life.

Have You Considered What Motivates People Have you ever considered what motivates others and yourself in terms of daily motivations and desires? Have You Determined Their Driving Forces Ever thought about what drives you? Whatever drives your hustling drive is also most likely driving others as well.

What drives you in life?

Understanding this million-dollar question can make a dramatic difference to both yourself and those closest to you - motivation being the force that keeps everything firmly in its place.

Finding out what motivates people is key to understanding them, yet this can be difficult due to everyone being different. One's past and present influences their goals that motivate them forward with life despite hardships they encounter along the way.

So in order to fully grasp what motivates people, it's necessary to get to know them individually. Through meeting with people directly and connecting on an intimate level, you can learn about their past experiences, the struggles they've overcome, key people in their life and any dreams or goals they hope to pursue in life - information which will allow you to piece together their personality that reveals their driving force in life.

According to researchers and psychologists, all people are born with three universal needs that drive them:

1. Independence -the motivation to make personal choices- is paramount, whilst 2. Proficiency provides motivation for being acknowledged for something.

3. Need for Connection--the Desire to Feel Valued By Others [3]

Hence, when trying to understand someone's motivations for change, pay close attention to the topics they bring up in conversation. Is their driving force their desire for control of affairs, finances, and other aspects of their life; or their desire to achieve higher positions at work with more competitive career goals; or perhaps it is simply being available and present for those in their life: friends, colleagues or family?

Talking with them will provide an indication of what motivates them. These three basic instincts may provide motivation; however, there are other forces which also spur motivation in individuals.

Some individuals prize fame and power. When you see high-power people such as politicians, business owners or union council leaders in positions such as politics or union council membership they likely are driven by moving further up in their career ladder. Others find motivation by taking on leadership roles within an institution or country bringing change through initiatives that improve things like service delivery or facilities management.

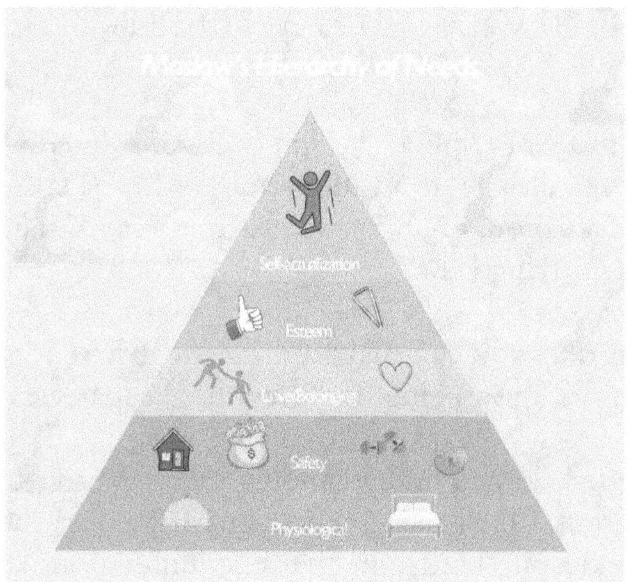

One can see this drive not only through their speech and actions but also in how they act. To connect with these types of individuals, be direct, factual and logical. They value their time highly; so they will respect you if you respect their time too.

Where some individuals are driven by external forces, others find motivation in intrinsic factors like passion. This could include traveling the world or working toward something that benefits others; people's eyes light up when discussing topics which excite their passion; often making sacrifices of sleep, leisure time or health for greater goals.

As soon as you connect with someone whose passion drives their actions, building an emotional bond should become easier. Understanding people's influences removes any guesswork about how best to understand them.

Maslow's Hierarchy of Needs)
In order to better comprehend human minds and emotions, Abraham Maslow (an American psychologist) developed a hierarchy of needs theory which illustrates basic needs as motivation drivers for people. This theory comprises five levels in its pyramid representation.

Once basic needs have been satisfied, one focuses on meeting additional levels until reaching the ultimate satisfaction and reaching the topmost level of their pyramid.

Maslow believed that people were motivated to meet their basic requirements before progressing toward more complex requirements.[4]

Let's dissect these five levels of hierarchy to gain a better understanding of what motivates individuals in life to progress further in their endeavors.

Level I: Physiological Needs of Students

These basic needs are essential to human survival and include:
* Water >> food.4vetement Clothing and shelter.
* Rest
At the base of the pyramid lies these needs which determine life or death. Even with strong relationships and self-confidence in place, without food for survival your existence would be in jeopardy - as would your relationships as your basic needs remain unmet you will likely seek other sources to fill that void - like trying to fill a square hole with round pegs!

Level Two of Maslow's Hierarchy of Needs Once we progress up Maslow's ladder of needs, safety and security become top priorities for those whose physiological needs have already been fulfilled. These needs arise out of a desire for control and order in life and include: * Health and Wellness * Financial Stability Initially these concerns might only have limited appeal but as you advance up Maslow's pyramid they become paramount considerations, such as for people whose physiological needs have already been satisfied
* Protection from injuries and accidents These needs compel individuals to obtain good employment with potential for advancement, secure health insurance, contribute towards savings accounts, and reside in secure neighborhoods for protection against theft and violence.

Maslow describes Level 3 of his hierarchy as including Love and Belongingness Needs as follows. These social needs include belongingness, acceptance and love - emotional needs which correspond with interpersonal connections and affiliations such as romantic relationships, friendships, social settings or community groups that satisfy these instincts.
* Religious Organizations
Feeling loved and appreciated by others is key to combatting feelings of loneliness, anxiety, depression and sadness. Attachments create the feeling of belonging in life by providing meaningful purpose - an emotional bond is vitally important in motivating human conduct at this stage of human evolution.

As we progress up Maslow's hierarchy of needs, requirements become more complicated. At this stage, esteem needs are the primary motivators in people - indulging their desire for respect and admiration is what fuels it all! People dedicate more of their time and efforts towards sports activities, professional accomplishments, academic successes or any other means which contribute towards satisfying self-esteem requirements.
People at this stage want to feel they are making a meaningful contribution to society and are valuable members. Achieved happiness means being satisfied with themselves,

which in turn empowers others around them. Positive influences in others' lives become important sources of validation for making other lives better.

People unable to meet this level of needs often develop an inferiority complex and are susceptible to low self-esteem issues; as a result, they believe they don't belong in relationships and that others would be better off without them. This in turn negatively affects interpersonal relationships as these feelings of inferiority tend to cause damage and damage interpersonal bonds as a result.

However, even needs that fall at the highest levels can still have an impactful influence on overall quality of life.

Level 5: Self-Actualization Needs

Once an individual's basic needs are satisfied, they can move onto meeting self-actualization needs by exploring their inner selves and applying their talents for personal growth. At this level, your ultimate aim should be achieving deep levels of fulfillment that will last throughout your lifetime.

No two people have the same idea of their ideal self, which influences their actions. Some focus on earning more money; others strive to make an impression in creative fields or volunteer for community services; still others seek inner fulfillment through self-development or giving back. Everyone longs to reach this ultimate satisfaction but setbacks often thwart progress - several individuals progress up the pyramid before finally arriving at this level of fulfillment.

Maslow identified this topmost level as "growth needs" while the four lower ones as "deficient needs." When striving to fulfill deficient needs, aspects may arise which lead to deprivation in various aspects such as food shortage, financial strain or feelings of isolation. By moving up each level in Maslow's hierarchy of needs hierarchy, unhappiness can be eliminated one step at a time.

On the contrary, if your level five needs aren't fulfilled, they won't lead to immediate hardship in terms of food, finances or security; rather they stem from your desire to develop yourself further as an individual and can have profoundly detrimental effects on your happiness levels.

Maslow's Theory often portrays itself as a rigid hierarchy; however, many have observed that its fulfillment does not follow an unwavering progression based on one's individual needs. For instance, some may prioritize self-esteem needs over love and acceptance needs, or perhaps creative accomplishment overshadows even fundamental necessities altogether; it all depends on an individual's priorities.

Maslow's Theory of Needs provides five core needs which comprise behavioral motivation. By understanding which step of the pyramid an individual falls, you can better comprehend them and communicate effectively.

T's called science because understanding something as complex as human behavior requires careful analysis of mind and behavior. Analyzing such studies provides you with tools to not only empathize with people but respond appropriately when they appear angry, sad, happy or experiencing any other emotion.

Have you ever considered Jung's Theory of Four Psychological Functions Have you ever found yourself questioning why some people seem more at home in large social gatherings while others flourish more when kept to smaller intimate settings? Have you wondered why some are always ready for fun while others long for an introspective night in with a book by the fire?

Because every individual's conscious energy and interests flow in different directions based on their personal psychological experiences and environmental influences, this theory was put forward by Swiss psychoanalyst and psychologist Carl Jung. According to him, certain attitudes and functions dominate in personality as opposing tendencies that determine its dominant personality type; these directions then determine its attitude type: introversion or extroversion.

Jung noted that dominant attitudes or functions become part of human consciousness while their opposite represent unconscious personality characteristics; such tendencies often surface under stress or through dreams.

Before we explore Jung's theory of four psychological functions, let's take a quick glance at two personality attitudes described by him that comprise its foundation.

Introversion vs. Extroversion--The Breakdown of Attitudes

Introversion and extroversion represent opposite ends of an attitude spectrum, determined by how one puts out energy. A person's orientation toward external factors also plays a part.

Introverts tend to withdraw their energy from objects and ensure external influences do not exert power on them; extroverts on the other hand tend to extend energy in an attempt to form active relationships with these objects. By definition, introverts focus on inner world while extroverts are focused more on external environments - psychologists today agree with Jung's theory that these temperaments can be genetically transmitted.

Jung's theory states that we tend to respond in four distinct ways based on our predominant personality attitudes: Thinking, Sensation, Intuition and Feeling.

He further divided these functions into two distinct groups: Rational (thinking and sensation) and Irrational (intuition and feeling).

Introversion and extroversion cannot be understood in isolation; rather they must be seen within context of these four functions to create a full picture of an individual's personality. This theory attempts to demonstrate the complexity of human typology.

Jung's theory holds that all four functions may become dominant at different times depending on external conditions; yet one function typically stands out due to inborn tendencies or developmental factors - this is how Jungian theory describes them.

Thinking: This form of evaluation relies upon logic and conceptual interdependencies between objects to assess truth or falsity of experiences, analyze reality through logic interference and analysis and make informed decisions. The process includes systematic and rational thought as it helps understand reality through systematic interplay and investigation.

Sensation: This function represents the aesthetic value assigned to an experience without any logical evaluation or reasoning; instead, sensations are perceived based on how things appear without hesitation; any concept such as context, meanings, implications or alternate interpretations is outside its purview and represents information exactly as it appears to the senses.

Intuition: The intuitive function is focused on our gut instinct or general perception of situations rather than detailed analysis or logical deduction. Intuition provides direction through its understanding of circumstances, relationships and latent possibilities in situations, without proof or evidence to back it up. Adding meaning to events through reading into situations intuitively while also picking up patterns that may be less noticeable right away is part of this function.

Feeling: Feeling is a sentimental function that involves evaluating a situation based on one's biases, likes and dislikes. Decisions are made based on past experiences that influence feelings about similar situations - which is always subjective.

Jung's theory of four psychological functions places rational and irrational functions at opposite ends of the spectrum (i.e., feeling is opposite thinking and intuition is opposite sensation), so that if sensation is your dominant function then intuition would not be included among your secondary functions; rather thinking and feeling would remain active decision makers unknowingly involved with decision-making processes.

Similar logic applies to personality traits (introversion and extroversion). If your predominant thinking mode is introverted, chances are your sub-conscious feeling mode will be extrovert.

People often find it challenging to use their secondary functions effectively, but through practice and awareness of your actions you can elevate these subliminal capabilities into conscious thought patterns.

Reading people can be done by knowing if their predominant functions lean towards being introverted or extroverted, which you can infer through common signs like their socializing preferences, expressiveness or social circle. Once this information has been established you can predict what function they typically use when making decisions.

Since the 1970s, psychiatrists have used Enneagram personality theory to identify individuals' characteristics and traits. It comprises a nine-point diagram in which each point represents one personality type which corresponds to how people think, feel, and act toward themselves and others. There are 27 subtypes within each point with three key centers representing feeling, action and thought which all influence our behaviors in different environments, ultimately being determined by our underlying motivations.

Enneagram seeks to characterize people based on their dominant motivations, fears, and behaviors in order to better understand an individual's personality. When reading people using Enneagram analysis, its personality types provide deeper insights into a person's strengths and weaknesses as well as how they relate to society as a whole. Furthermore, Enneagram helps understand motivations behind why individuals act the way they do.

The Enneagram theory asserts that people are born with one dominant personality type, yet this can change due to experiences and external factors. External and inborn traits tend to influence each other; instinctive personality characteristics determine how someone responds in stressful situations; which in turn shapes their personality into either being anxious or calm.

This theoretical system further emphasizes the fact that people do not fit neatly into one category; their personalities instead comprise of multiple traits combining basic types, with some additional "wings," known as temperament modifiers or wings. Although wings have some influence over temperament, they do not significantly change dominant personality types; according to this theory, basic traits tend to remain constant over time, though specific ones may change due to external influences like habits and health.

Individuals may possess several personality traits, with the dominant type always standing out as being most significant to them. An Enneagram test can help identify these personality traits.

Now, let us consider: what are the nine personality types found within the Enneagram of personality? Let's examine them further.

Enneagram Type 1--Principled Reformers People belonging to this personality type are driven by the desire to act morally and ethically righteously. They value integrity, principles, self-control and perfection in all areas of life. Type Ones tend to be accepting towards both themselves and those around them while striving for self-mastery and excellence in all spheres of their life. They tend to be accepting towards both themselves and those close to them but at times may become intolerant and judgmental when their imperfections surface or make them feel inadequate or inadequate themselves.

Type Ones typically inhabit the action center of the Enneagram, though their action and control tend to come from within - through principles, discipline, and self-discipline.

These principles serve as their guiding force and make Ones appear organized and quality-focused.

People belonging to this category tend to possess an acute sense of right and wrong, setting high standards both for themselves and the people around them. Their inner dialogue often features lots of "I must" or "I should" statements as they keep an internal scorecard against themselves, potentially leading to expansion and contraction in their lives.

Ones are known for experiencing frequent bouts of anger, though they typically keep it under control. Their anger usually manifests itself through resentment or irritation when others engage in irresponsible or unethical behavior; in extreme cases it manifests into passive-aggressive behaviour where their physical rigidity increases while they become unusually polite despite being critical of others and often seem nonreceptive about criticism from outside sources, leading them down the path toward frustration and eventually anger.

Type Ones are relatively rare - according to one study with over 54,000 respondents, only 10% make up Type Ones.[6]

Enneagram Type 2--Considerate Helpers
Type Twos have an inherent desire to feel cherished by the people around them, placing great importance on cultivating meaningful connections and generosity, kindness, and selflessness. Their goal is to make the world a loving environment by giving support and attention to those closest to them.

At their best, Type Twos can be warm, affectionate, and generous individuals who share modesty and humility with the world. Unfortunately, less-healthy Twos may appear self-centered and manipulative, giving just for a reward; their inner voice tells them they're only worthwhile if others love and need them and this may prompt them to overextend themselves and give more than necessary.

Twos' action patterns are driven by their desire to develop relationships. Therefore, they exert energy and effort into forging close ties and friendships, drawing people in with generous gestures of praise or compliments that make others feel special and appreciated. Twos tend to provide excellent advice-giving services as quickly as they respond when someone needs assistance, or sense that someone could potentially harm those they care about.

Twos' thought processes are guided by consideration and thoughtfulness. They're attuned to others' needs - even those unaware of their desires - which makes their thoughts often consumed by other people and how to connect with them in meaningful ways. As a result, a significant portion of mental energy may be dedicated to trying to connect.

Twos tend to take great pleasure in feeling indispensable, which may translate to prideful self-regard or an exaggerated sense of their own importance and ultimately undermine interpersonal relationships.

Twos' feelings tend to manifest externally as warm and supportive energy. Their strong empathy makes them adept at sensing others' emotions and responding accordingly, and while generally friendly towards people they can sometimes surprise with their heightened anger when feeling they have been ignored or treated unfairly; Twos are assertive when protecting those they care about when they perceive being treated unfairly and experience emotional pain if being disregarded or ignored.

Type Twos make up approximately 11 percent of the population, with women being more prevalent within that percentage than men.

Enneagram Type 3--Competitive Achiever

Competitive achievers are motivated by a desire to outdo themselves and exceed previous achievements with greater ones. Results, recognition and efficiency become of utmost importance in their eyes, leading them to adapt their actions according to circumstances in order to reach new levels of achievements.

At their best, these individuals can be seen as principled, hardworking, and motivated individuals, spreading integrity and hope throughout the world. However, at times their desire for success may consume them to such an extent that it leads them away from important relationships in life - making them feel particularly self-important and increasing their sense of self worth through actions rather than words.

Doers tend to act with goal-oriented action plans. Their energy and focus is directed toward accomplishing tasks efficiently. Many belonging to this personality type can easily change their persona to fit whatever behavior, role, or expectations are expected of them; their competitive nature often manifests itself during recreational activities or at work - individuals in this personality type tend to find activities or competitions which allow them to shine more while social Threes prefer team competitions as opportunities to show leadership qualities within groups - appearing energetic and confident at any given time.

Threes' thinking patterns give their personalities an optimistic edge. They see failures as opportunities to learn rather than let them hold them back from moving forward with their goals. Threes tend to emphasize information which supports their point of view while disregarding others. Their success lies in their ability to focus on the right things and make calculated decisions; their quick thought process allows them to quickly grasp any situation quickly before adapting with appropriate communication and engagement skills to make things go according to plan.

Their competition arises from their desire to compare themselves with others and judge themselves on how well or poorly they compare, often becoming totally immersed in their work, until it becomes part of who they are as an individual.

Their feeling patterns allow them to emotionally disengage from any situation and make objective, rational decisions. Their negative emotions--such as stress, fear and anxiety--don't consume them, yet they still experience frustration and anger.

Threes aim to avoid getting on people's bad side whenever possible if it can contribute to their success in any way. They are aware of how people may respond to their attitudes and actions; although they may appear friendly from the outside, inside they could feel distrustful of others; their focus lies in projecting confidence to others, thus suppressing anything which takes their focus away from doing this; others may perceive Threes as unmoved or even serious due to this behaviour.

Enneagram Type Threes are among the rarest personality types. Out of 54,000 participants who took part in a study mentioned earlier, only 11% identified with this personality type; most identified themselves as male.

Enneagram Type 4--Intense Creative

Enneagram Type Fours are driven to express their unique creativity through words, work or any other outlet - including language itself! As they value individualism they place great importance on self-expression and feelings.

Romantics at heart and admirers of beauty, Fours are true creatives in the truest sense. At their best, those belonging to this category are sensitive yet content, with an authentic flair that makes them one-of-a-kind; at worst they may come off as temperamental or melancholic due to being aware of their flaws and wounds; their self-talk involves seeking purpose in life by expressing themselves authentically.

Fours' actions are driven by their need to express themselves. They thrive by sharing profound experiences with those they care for, often by drawing out their inner artist or using symbols. Their eccentric personality often leaves them frustrated and disenchanted when performing tedious tasks that don't fulfil their desires.

Fours tend to use statements like, "I,", "me,", and "mine," which share personal experiences with an audience. While this may appear self-absorbed at first, this is actually their way of connecting with others and building relationships.

Your thinking patterns stem from your need to fill any holes in your life, like missing pieces of yourself. They tend to internalize negative information about themselves while disregarding positive data - leading them to internalize negative messages about themselves while dismissing any positive news, which in turn may trigger reactions whenever someone suggests negative implications about them. Their judgment becomes clouded by emotions as their judgment relies heavily on emotions rather than logic - this often results in making biased decisions due to this bias in judgment based on experience or emotional connections forming the basis for making important decisions.

Fours' introspective nature tends to lead them down an internal road of thoughts that is sometimes too deep for their comfort, leading them down negative thought paths which ultimately diminish their self-esteem and lead them into being misunderstood by other people.

Fours' feelings are their greatest asset; they help them feel connected to the world and others alike. Additionally, Fours are acutely aware of others' emotions - often more so than themselves! Unfortunately, Fours tend to dwell too long on their emotions which makes them appear deep, intense, and moody.

Fours believe that experiencing their emotions - whether sadness or happiness - allows them to explore who they truly are. Their emotions often fluctuate with changes in the world around them, although sadness, longing, and loss tend to impact more heavily than happiness and can make them appear melancholic or distant from society. Unfortunately they often take things too seriously and need some lightheartedness in their lives.

Type Four individuals tend to be unique individuals who stand out from the crowd with their individualistic style and flair, often making them stand out in crowd. [7]

Enneagram Type 5--Quiet Investigator

Fives are known for their introspective nature, driven by an internal desire to uncover truth and understand others for making decisions. When trying to comprehend their environment, Fives place great value in knowledge and objectivity when making decisions based on objective knowledge. Fives also prioritize independence over anything else and remain conscious of financial savings as opposed to asking others for assistance or asking others for support when making financial decisions; furthermore they respect privacy by giving others enough room to live.

Others often view Fives as wise and visionaries, with non-attachments that enable meaningful connections with people. At their worst, Fives may appear intelligently arrogant or disconnected from their emotions as they often retreat into introspective states to try and make sense of the world around them.

Fives focus their actions around enjoying solitude and their own company, placing great importance on "privacy," although each individual may define it differently. They use alone time to recharge resources and set boundaries with others while being independent - this often includes making changes to routines or surroundings to maintain autonomy without becoming dependent. These changes could involve adopting minimalist lifestyles or hoarding on one extreme or the other end.

Fives tend to be conservative with how they utilize available resources as this can hinder their independence. They may appear distant or disinterested until something of interest to them comes up - at which time you will find them being highly responsive and communicative, sharing information with others.

Thinking is at the core of their being, as they strongly believe in knowledge being power. Their thirst for knowledge drives them to explore information in depth; should something catch their interest, they would go to any lengths to master it and establish themselves as experts in that domain.

Mind is a sacred space where they can find solace from the rest of life. People with this talent can organize information into various compartments in their mind - be it events, dates or any other facts - in order to maintain interest in various topics while creating clear boundaries between various aspects of relationships and life.

Their emotional states are greatly influenced by their cerebral capacity, as they tend to understand their emotions by intellectualizing and trusting in their minds to make sense of them. Unfortunately, this makes it hard for them to separate between feelings and thoughts, which often leaves them exhausted after emotionally charged events or open-ended projects.

One can become exhausted when continually managing personal resources and energy, yet their ability to detach from feelings can help manage energy more effectively. By detaching themselves, they gain power over when to review or relive feelings at their convenience, which allows for further emotional processing at their convenience. Their emotional distancing behavior serves two functions - it allows them to control emotions more easily as well as protecting against hurt and pain; unfortunately this coping mechanism sometimes causes them to appear cold or distant from others; yet this strategy makes for an introspective and balanced personality.

Type Fives are rare personality types. A survey with 54,000 correspondents revealed that only 10% of participants fall into this personality type on average, and it is more prevalent among men compared to women (14% for male participants and 7% for female ones).

Enneagram Type 6--Loyal Skeptic Sixes are driven by a strong desire for belonging and security; this drives their decisions and relationships. As they strive for safety in every situation, sixes value people who demonstrate loyalty while being responsible; they often exhibit courage while being deeply connected with themselves - giving those around them gifts of trust and devotion in exchange. Unhealthy sixes tend to worry excessively while letting fear lower their defenses, leaving them appearing suspicious, doubting, or anxious.

Their inner self-talk tells them that the world can be an unsafe and cruel place, so being prepared and loyal to those you care about are key ingredients of survival. They strive not to fear what awaits them out there and remain guarded, always looking out for themselves against its cruelty.

Sixes typically exhibit one of two action patterns. Either they display fear and avoidance behavior to avoid emotionally overwhelming situations or they attempt to confront anxiety head on by facing it head on. Most Sixes fall somewhere in-between these extremes; their behavior will change depending on circumstances in their lives.

Certain people belonging to this personality type often engage in risk-taking behavior to prove to themselves and others that they are courageous and fearless, whether that manifests as risky adventures or verbal acts against people with counterphobic patterns. Sixes are known for working diligently, consistently, with dedication and consistency while placing great value on responsibility, loyalty, and fully dedicating themselves to any task at hand. Their admirable work ethics make them valuable employees, which makes other people comfortable handing over projects to them.

Sixes tend to avoid issues when possible. When faced with an unpleasant situation, however, their thinking patterns motivate them to analyze threats and risks critically in order to stay attuned with their surroundings and recognize all possible challenges and problems that might arise. Though they have the capability of solving their own problems quickly and efficiently, their response may sometimes include "yes, but" which makes for difficult communication among all parties involved.

People with this personality type are aware of their authority in their thinking. While they feel protected and supported by authority figures, they also worry about being let down or disappointed by others. Their thought process involves asking themselves internal questions that serve as "internal committees", with many unexpressed emotions explored alongside obvious ones.

Their feelings often center around anxiety as they focus on worst-case scenarios in daily dealings, often experiencing panic or mild worry; or more intense forms like terror and dread. Their emotional response allows for quick access at any time; but unfortunately this means replaying worryful scenarios in their minds even when things are going well for them in life; tending to discount positive emotions while dwelling on negative ones instead.

By being deeply attuned with their feelings, many people tend to unconsciously project their emotions, hopes, thoughts and fears onto those in front of them. Their own doubts and insecurities often manifest into difficult behaviour that causes problems for others.

People with Types Six personalities can be recognized by their ability to fit seamlessly into any environment and always strive to support those closest to them.

Enneagram Type 7--Enthusiastic Visionary
People belonging to personality type Seven are extremely enthusiastic about life, always motivated to maximize its enjoyment while avoiding conflicting situations. By nature, Sevens tend to be optimists - always searching out opportunities that inspire them in life and capitalize on these possibilities when available. They see life as an adventure which drives their spontaneity and appreciation of everything around them; although others might perceive Sevens as calm when in "present mode", as they find enjoyment from spontaneous activities; due to this spontaneous nature they might appear uncommitted or even unfocused due to their desire for adrenaline rush from living!

Their behaviors focus on finding ways to escape routine and monotony in their lives, so they actively search out activities or people that add excitement and adventure. Never afraid to try new things, they sometimes abandon unfinished tasks for more exciting ventures.

Sevens strive to stay active, and move confidently forward. Their energy lies in embracing every challenge with gusto; that rush of adrenaline that comes from every burst of excitement keeps them going strong. Under pressure, this personality type may switch plans or multitask in order to complete tasks successfully. Their bodies can often outrun their minds when taking on new endeavors - this means their high energy levels often appear as constant movement or busy body language - giving others the impression they are restless but this is simply their way of staying engaged!

Sevens' thinking patterns are driven by an active mind that fluidly transitions between ideas and connections effortlessly, engaging them to explore what piques their interest and brings instantaneous gratification. Therefore, their thinking patterns involve fast mental processing and stimulation combined. Sevens are inclined toward having plenty of options and dislike feeling restricted in any regard; having options provides them with freedom; their quick wit allows them to gain knowledge across many fields which encourages innovation and creativity as they have plenty of data at their fingertips to draw from.

Also, they relish sharing their ideas with others as this keeps them feeling inspired and engaged with life. When new information arrives, they tend to grasp it quickly while discovering even more along the way.

Sevens tend to experience positive emotional landscapes that manifest themselves through energetic and upbeat personalities, leading others to view Sevens as optimistic, joyful, and enthusiastic individuals. When facing negative emotions like boredom, sadness, anxiety or fear they instinctively look for ways to turn these negative feelings around quickly so as to escape discomfort more quickly.

Sevens' natural tendency toward positive emotions often causes them to view negative experiences with optimism by framing them as learning experiences or opportunities in their minds. Unfortunately, this rationalization makes taking responsibility for actions when things go south more difficult; but on the plus side it keeps their outlook positive and helps maintain an optimistic perspective of life.

Sevens tend to be highly protective of their personal space and don't appreciate being challenged about their abilities. If you challenge a Seven, prepare to face their wrath. When confronted with uncomfortable or heavy situations, Sevens work tirelessly to lighten the mood with jokes or make lighthearted statements to ease tensions and restore equilibrium by engaging in laughter-inducing anecdotes.

The Truity study discovered that Enneagram Type Sevens comprised 9 percent of respondents surveyed out of 54,000 participants.[8]

Enneagram Type 8-Active Challenger Type Eights are driven by their need to appear strong and avoid showing vulnerability as much as possible, leading them to be direct and impactful in dealing with situations they find themselves involved in. They quickly take control of situations by controlling it with directness. Eights thrive when challenged and are fair in their dealings, using their righteous sense of justice to safeguard others. At their best, Eights appear deeply caring yet strong yet approachable. When Eights act in line with reality, they gift us all with innocence. However, at their worst Eights may appear aggressive, domineering, and lustful as part of their strategy to appear larger than life in an often cruel world. By controlling situations they believe they can navigate around injustices more easily.

Eights reside at the heart of Enneagram. They're at its core, taking action based on instinct rather than doing nothing at all, often manifested through intense and direct speech, choice of words, body language and decision-making style. Eights love taking control and making things happen on their own terms; their independence allows them to pursue projects they find fulfilling.

Cooperating with others doesn't come naturally to Eights; they do it out of obligation. Eights take pride in maintaining control, often micromanaging events themselves and often end up micromanaging others when necessary. Their quick actions serve them well when other become overwhelmed and become unruly - they quickly step in, take charge, and resolve things efficiently without hesitation or delay.

Micromanaging may not be their favorite activity, but it keeps them in control of the situation and generates results - thus they do whatever needs to be done to meet this end.

Eights do not tolerate incompetence and weakness in those they take responsibility for, yet are fiercely protective of those under their stewardship. When someone they care about is being treated unfairly, Eights will fight tirelessly to uphold justice and right any injustices done to them.

Eights tend to categorize people as weak or strong and act accordingly, often paying more attention to certain individuals based on this "all or nothing" assessment method. Eights tend to favor honesty over ambiguity when handling conflictual situations, preferring truth over remaining out of the loop as this makes them feel powerless over the situation; equipping themselves with as much information about updates, progress or events helps Eights focus on the bigger picture more efficiently.

Staying focused on their own motives more than those of others is key for these people; they don't appreciate being forced into doing things they don't enjoy or find boring, because this wastes their energy inefficiently.

Eights have complex emotional patterns. They tend to get angry quickly and react accordingly, yet after venting their ire quickly they quickly move on from it. Because Eights seek to avoid feeling vulnerable they tend not to express feelings of sadness or weakness openly - instead preferring instead to recognize these feelings only when safe - showing love through power and protection as part of their identity.

The Truity study with 54,000 participants demonstrated that 15% of people fall within Enneagram Type Eight; these people were predominantly men.

Enneagram Type 9--Adaptive Peacemaker

Nines tend to act as mediators, driven by a desire to create harmony in their surroundings. As such, they strive to be accepting and accommodating of those around them while prioritizing peacemaking in all they do - this enables them to avoid conflict whenever possible.

Most of the world perceives Nines as vibrant, experienced, and self-aware individuals who strive to deliver actions that benefit those around them. At worst, however, Nines may appear stubborn, lazy, or self-denying; this happens because they go along with everyone in order to maintain peace but then value other's needs over their own needs and create feelings of discomfort for themselves and those they interact with. Yet their complacent nature attracts others towards them while also making people feel at ease when in their presence.

Nines tend to take action based on their desire to avoid others' control by either manipulating their environment or passively resisting when something doesn't feel comfortable. Their actions or lack thereof will likely be driven by maintaining peace and harmony as they cannot tolerate conflict.

Comfort can be found through familiar routines and rhythms they find intriguing, while this personality type enjoys forging meaningful connections that result in the merging of energies from people close to them, often manifesting itself through adopting the habits or interests of those present within their intimate spaces.

Nines' thinking patterns lend themselves well to structured processes; therefore, they prioritize details and clarity when approaching tasks or creating habits or procedures quickly. When presented with large volumes of information, Nines will quickly organize it in their minds into an orderly structure to make sense of it all.

Nines tend to be strong-willed and persistent, yet tend to keep their opinions to themselves, in order to avoid appearing overbearing to others. Unfortunately, this leaves them discontented with some aspects of their relationships or lives.

Their attitude may appear relaxed and level-headed, yet they experience intense emotions with great intensity, necessitating effort on their part to control them and appear peaceful, serene and approachable. Their intense emotions motivate them to maintain harmony among people because they understand how feelings influence behavior.

Though they excel as peaceful mediators in conflict situations, Nines tend to avoid engaging with negative emotions like anger directly; such connections tend to drain them of energy and they don't often acknowledge these feelings either. Therefore, they try not to experience them too intensely. Furthermore, most Nines are empaths who can sense emotions from those close to them, often picking up on energy shared between people if their surroundings are positive and enthusiastic; conversely when faced with sad or anxious individuals their mood may also decrease dramatically.

Ninth grade students comprise 13% of respondents in the Truity study; most of which are women.

The nine personality types represented on the Enneagram wheel can be divided into Heart, Head and Body types. Heart types consist of types two through four that rely on emotional intelligence for navigation through life and connecting with people around them; Head types include types five through seven that rely on intellectual processing of situations; while Body types one through nine utilize instincts and gut feelings when responding in situations.

Researchers throughout history have explored various methodologies for understanding human personality. One such test, known as The Big Five Personality Test (OCEAN), uses Big Five Factor Markers derived from Goldberg's International Personality Item Pool introduced in 1992 as a factor analysis method to explore statistical responses of groups by answering this question: What's an ideal way of summarizing someone's personality?"[9]

Though personality variables cannot be quantified, answers categorize individuals into five broad groups according to their dominant traits: (O-Openness C-Conscientiousness D-Extroversion E- Extroversion A- Agreeableness

N - Neuroticism By understanding these personality types, you can better comprehend people by understanding their needs, building meaningful connections through common interests and tailoring your behavior accordingly.

An interesting factor here is that these personalities can be the product of both nature and nurture. Parents may pass them down, or individuals can develop them from how they were raised.

Let's delve deeper into these personality traits and assess whether nature or nurture has the greater influence.

Openness This personality trait is known for being welcoming of new knowledge and experiences. People rated higher on this scale tend to be insightful and imaginative with many interests that vary widely; innovation and curiosity also feature prominently within them; on the other hand those ranking lower may be more cautious, consistent, and struggle with abstract thought processes. If you want to gauge someone's level of openness on a scale like this one, try asking these questions: Do you love adventure?

Does your imagination run wild? Have you been the one initiating new activities before?

Are You Prepared for New Challenges?

Answering "yes" to all these questions indicates high openness levels. People with such high openness levels relish being challenged in life and look for creative outlets through which to express themselves creatively. 57% of individuals heritably possess this trait of openness.

Conscientiousness

General characteristics of this personality trait include goal-oriented behavior, thoughtfulness and good impulse control. Conscientious people tend to be great planners and think ahead when making life decisions; furthermore they are highly aware of how their actions impact others as well as deadlines that may need meeting.

People who rank highly on the conscientiousness scale tend to be attentive, organized and efficient in their approach to tasks and details. People who rank lower are usually laid-back and relaxed. Here are a few questions that will help you assess where a person stands in terms of conscientiousness:

Do You Take Pride In Being Self Disciplined?

Are You Organized and Prepared for Whatever May Arise? Or would You Prefer Being Spontaneous Instead? Are You Enjoy Keeping To A Schedule, Prioritizing Tasks Promptly and Paying Attention To Details Immediately?

Answering "yes" to these questions indicates a high level of conscientiousness within an individual, as demonstrated by organization and order in life and relationships. Conscientiousness has 49% hereditary influence.

Extroverted traits can be identified by characteristics like sociability, assertiveness, excitement, emotional expressiveness and talkativeness. People exhibiting this personality trait tend to be outgoing and thrive when participating in social gatherings.

People who score highly on the extrovert scale thrive by being at the center of attention and enjoying being around people. By contrast, people who score low (introverts) find social interactions exhausting and enjoy solitude more than other people's company.

To understand extroversion in someone, ask the following questions: 8.5 Do you experience difficulty being the focus of attention at gatherings or initiating conversation in social settings? Do you enjoy meeting new people and do you possess a large circle of acquaintances or friends?

Do you tend to voice things before giving them any thought?

If they agree with these questions, they score highly on the extroversion scale. If you find yourself around people who score lower on this scale, try not to force them into becoming extroverts by encouraging excessive talking or pushing them into social gatherings; those with introverted personality traits tend to stick closer to those and places which provide emotional nourishment and comfort.

Extrovert traits have 54% hereditary influence.

Agreeableness

This personality dimension encompasses attributes of kindness, trust, affection, altruism and other prosocial characteristics. Individuals high in agreeableness tend to be compassionate, friendly and cooperative while those low in this trait may become detached, analytical or competitive, sometimes even reaching into manipulative behavior.

Question individuals to ascertain where they stand on the agreeableness scale: Do they trust easily and readily extend second chances to others, are they empathic, do they like making others comfortable, etc.

Are you passionate about providing assistance to those in need?

An affirmative answer to these questions indicates a high rank on the agreeableness scale. Individuals scoring low on this scale often don't experience empathy naturally and must make conscious efforts and changes in behavior in order to put themselves in other people's shoes and react accordingly; 42% of hereditary factors play a part in agreeableness traits.

Neuroticism Attributed to this personality dimension are traits such as moodiness, emotional instability and sadness. Neuroticism refers to how someone handles their emotions; people scoring highly on this scale tend to be sensitive, easily irritable and susceptible to mood swings; on the other hand those scoring lower tend to be emotionally secure, secure and resilient.

By asking these questions, it is possible to assess where someone stands on the neuroticism scale: (Worrisome? Easy Stress Out? Recurrent Shifts In Mood)

Do you find it difficult to deal with stressful situations?

Answering in the affirmative to these questions indicates high neuroticism in a person. Knowing their triggers and calmers will be beneficial in keeping their mood under control.

Neuroticism has a 48% hereditary component.

Understanding these characteristics and how they influence people is the key to better communication and determining how best to interact with someone in front of you.

Dr. David Keirsey's Temperament Theory

An educational creator and psychologist, Dr. David Keirsey introduced the Keirsey Temperament Sorter that categorizes individuals into four temperament groups based on activity patterns, communication habits, character attitudes, talents and values - taking into account each person's impact in the workplace relative to personal needs.

Dr. David Kersey states that human personality can be divided into four broad groups based on temperament. Each temperament includes its own set of strengths, weaknesses and qualities that characterize its characteristics. These four temperaments include:

Artisans These people can easily be distinguished from others by their expertise in creative fields like arts, literature and poetry. Their actions serve as expression of their artistry while their sense of adventure propels them towards taking risks or being spontaneous at times.

Guardians occupy an essential position within society by cooperating with those around them and following rules espoused by traditional cultures. Their dedication is what helps keep order intact - they constitute 40 to 45% of population members.

Idealist People who focus on self-growth and improvement likely belong to the Idealist temperament group, with strong senses of loyalty to others, motivated to take actions which help others, and actively taking steps that benefit society as a whole. Between 15-20% of the population belongs to this temperament category.

Rationals, known for their pragmatic and logical thinking styles, are among the rarest of personality types and renowned for their problem-solving expertise. Once something captures their imagination, however, they may become so immersed that they become detached from reality that others perceive them as strange or distant.

Only 5- 10% of the population falls into the Rationals temperament group. Career counselors frequently utilize Keirsey Temperament Sorter as it assists people in understanding themselves better and leading them down the right career path.

All these theories aim to understand human nature, what motivates individuals, and their response to certain situations. With knowledge accumulated by researchers over decades, we are better able to read people and forge connections between us all.

As most people believe, listening does not equate to hearing. People usually enter conversations either hoping to be heard or hoping not to be heard altogether - the latter case often leads us to pay less attention to what the other person is saying than we intended, with both parties experiencing our lack of interest as being felt by both sides.

Listening intently can be a game-changer in conversations and your ability to understand people. Simply paying attention to what people actually say could change everything: no need for guessing how someone thinks; simply listen carefully when someone speaks if you want a peek inside someone's head; instead pay more attention when someone speaks; many don't hide their thoughts and opinions behind walls of steel, preferring instead being open about who they are and are unafraid to let you in if only you listen intently enough!

You won't feel the need to read someone's mind if you can accurately interpret their intentions when speaking.

Carl Rogers and Richard Farson first popularized the term "active listening" in 1957, and its definition became widely recognized over time. Active and passive listening are two forms of listening. For the best listening results, one should prioritize active listening. To truly focus on someone, one needs to prioritize active listening over passive.

Active listening requires mental presence, patience and the ability to hear without feeling like one must speak in response. Focus on understanding what the other person is communicating while resisting any urges to interrupt. Every time you feel you have something better to add, decide to wait. Each time we speak we miss an opportunity for growth. By giving someone safe space to express themselves you may gain valuable insight. Allow someone else hold your hand as they lead you on an intimate tour through their mind!

No need for guessing and reading between the lines! Just let the other person talk without interruptions or judgments - this way you will discover more about them than with any other strategy!

People love talking about themselves! Take advantage of this natural tendency by showing genuine interest and asking probing questions to uncover all that information about themselves that they might reveal.

Use Body Language for Support
Talking with someone whose eyes are fixed on nothing behind your shoulder is neither pleasant nor encouraging, so make sure your body language echoes your interest when communicating. Turn towards them, smile frequently and nod frequently while maintaining eye contact - don't look bored or disinterested as this will quickly become evident and be disrespectful of them as you learn more about their identity.

Reducing Distractions

It is essential that your mind remains free from distraction. While someone else is speaking, resist the urge to make mental lists or respond to emails during that conversation; be present. Anything which causes distraction should be removed: move your phone away from direct line of sight so it does not tempt you to pick it up or check notifications every time it rings!

Nod Encouragedly and Respond to Their Stories

Be sure to nod encouragingly, lean forward, and respond appropriately when hearing stories so as to convey that you're deeply invested while not overdoing it so as to look forceful. There are various ways you can demonstrate you're listening; here are a few:

* Respond using your body. For instance, opening your eyes wider or tightening fists could act as a clue that something is amiss - be it shock, surprise, disappointment or excitement.

* Restate their statement. For example, if they tell you they prefer carrots over other vegetables in general, responding with something like, "You mean to say of all the vegetables on earth you prefer carrots?" To show that you were paying attention, repeat what they said out loud so the other person knows you heard and understood their point. This shows your interest and shows them you care.

* Ask them to repeat themselves. Although this might appear rude, doing so shows your respect for every word they share and ensures you don't miss anything important.

Simply listening can help you gain much more knowledge about people than any other approach could. When we listen when someone speaks and pose pertinent questions, we may learn so much more than otherwise! Show genuine interest in others and they'll open their brain games for you to explore!

Have you ever gone on a date and been left pondering what the other person was thinking or feeling? Ideally there would be signs to let us know the progress of meeting. Well... there is! Body language is an unconscious means of conveying how someone is feeling; to interpret its cues properly. Sometimes these subconscious signals come to light unknowingly. UCLA research[12] illustrates this point; only 7% of communication takes place through what we say (i.e., words), 38% via tone and 55% using body language - learning to interpret this 55% can give an edge when understanding people.

So the next time you go on a date or attend any social gathering, keep an eye out for these subtle cues:

* Smiling Eyes: They say eyes are the window to our souls; that is certainly true! When people are happy, their smile can often escape hiding despite attempts at hiding it, until eventually their skin crinkles around their eyes, creating crow's feet--revealing its presence! Sometimes people smile just out of politeness or to hide true feelings--so if you want to know if someone's genuine smiling, just pay attention to their eyes!

*Crossed legs and arms: Crossing one's legs and arms forms a physical barrier against those standing before them and indicates resistance, even when their words or smile indicate otherwise. Psychological interpretation suggests this body language indicates someone emotionally, psychologically, or physically removed from whatever lies before them.

* Raised Brows: When someone raises their eyebrows, it could indicate worry, fear or surprise. It's hard to do in casual conversation; try raising them while enjoying coffee with your friends and you'll notice the difference immediately.

* Mirroring Body Language: Have you ever encountered someone mirroring your body language by tilting their head the same way or uncrossing their legs at exactly the same moment that you do? This shows that they're interested in what you are saying and are subconsciously copying you unknowingly out of respect; should this happen on a date, this could be invaluable!

* Clenched Jaw: When engaging in conflict or dispute situations, one characteristic that becomes evident quickly is someone's clenched jaw, furrowed brow or tightened neck - because being uncomfortable triggers physical tension in their body that manifests into stress signals that cause this reaction.

* Exaggerated nodding: If someone responds by nodding repeatedly in response to what you are saying, this doesn't indicate their agreement with what is being said - rather it shows anxiety on their behalf and their desire to please you by nodding accordingly.

Even though you can't read someone's mind directly, you can still observe their body language and interpret their true feelings. Learning the psychology of people is a lifelong learning journey that only gets better with experience. Unlocking motivations behind their actions and correlating them with personality traits provides deeper insights into how our minds work and how you can untangle it.

PART THREE: WHAT YOU SHOULD BRING TO THE TABLE

Have you ever considered how your contributions impact a conversation? Understanding people requires not just watching what others do but observing the actions themselves as well. Communication is two-way; to tread properly you need to do your part by understanding and aligning yourself to what the other party is communicating to you.

No one can accurately read people if you are filled with prejudices and beliefs that prevent you from seeing the full picture. Before beginning to observe others, it is necessary to gain an in-depth knowledge of yourself - how you act, think, and perceive people.

This section explores your internal beliefs to ascertain if any biases, prejudices, or limited understanding of human nature are hindering communication or perceptions of others.

Remember when Donald Trump tweeted "I'm a very stable genius"? His response drew criticism from comedians and journalists for lacking self-awareness, yet most people fail in this area, often leading to difficulty understanding others. While it might sound confusing at first, "every person is your mirror," so to fully comprehend another individual, you first need to fully comprehend yourself! This is something most people are unaware of!

This leads us into our next question (i.e., how to know yourself). Well, it's an extensive process that involves being brutally honest with yourself - sometimes this may sound easy or easy, but sometimes this challenge becomes the greatest one of all your life! For example, sometimes our anger or emotional outbursts may seem justified because other people triggered them; yet it is our responsibility as individuals to control our reactions instead of assigning blame to them.

Blind spots are defined as traits visible to others but invisible to ourselves. A psychologist named Simine Vazire conducted an experiment to test this theory.[13] He asked participants to assess themselves and four friends on various traits such as intelligence, emotional stability, assertiveness and creativity to see who could more accurately predict who predicted each person's personality and traits better: either themselves or their friends. The goal was to ascertain which predicted personality more accurately.

Results revealed that people were more aware of their own emotional stability compared to that of their friends, such as when speaking in public or how stressed they appear when speaking up in group discussions. Friends had better insight into whether an assertive candidate participated or predicted their performance on creativity or IQ tests.

Your ability to understand your emotional bandwidth shows in its greater visibility to others than it might otherwise.

Traits that are more visible to other people than to yourself may remain mysterious to you. Singing at a karaoke bar requires convincing both yourself and those listening that your talent exists, yet these listeners can best assess your singing style and vocal range.

People tend to overestimate their intelligence, with this pattern more commonly observed among men than women. People also tend to overestimate how generous they actually are since generosity is seen as admirable trait. People also mistakenly believe they are not biased or judgmental because who would admit such claims against themselves?

How can you clear this fuzzy view of yourself and see yourself clearly in the mirror? Whenever an aspect of yourself is difficult for you to accept, ask those closest to you for support in holding up a mirror for you. Friends, parents or romantic partners tend to have more insight into who you really are than anyone else; yet their impression can also become clouded due to love or biases they hold against you.

Your VITALS make up your personality; understand them. These include:

Values (V), Interests (I), Temperament (T), Around-the-Clock Activities and Goals (ATC), Life Mission and Goals (LMG), are important for successful living.

S - Skills/Strengths

Recognizing your values - such as helping others, being honest, being kind - forms the basis for making important life decisions and setting goals. Knowing your values keeps you going when times get tough and keeps motivation high! Writing these down in a journal or diary has proven to motivate actions taken towards self-awareness! Knowing thy values!

* When making decisions, do you rely on feelings or facts? * How do you recharge your energy stores--extrovert or introvert? * Do you plan everything out meticulously or go with the flow? * Are details more important to you or larger ideas?

Understanding your responses to such queries will allow you to intuitively place yourself in situations that will foster growth while avoiding those which limit it. When your personality aligns with its surrounding environment, energy is used for productive projects rather than being wasted away and you feel less exhausted than before.

Biorhythms or around-the-clock activities: Here, the focus should be on your biorhythms or around-the-clock activities, for instance when do you experience your peak energy levels: morning or mid-day? Harmonizing with your biology allows you to schedule activities when they will give the greatest returns; often these characteristics have been present since birth - it's just a matter of recognizing them and acting upon them accordingly.

Combining biological frequencies with activities brings rewarding experiences, making life much simpler when you don't pretend to be someone you aren't!

Life becomes happier and more meaningful when we understand our life's missions and goals. If you're uncertain how to go about doing this, think back on events that were especially meaningful in your life, examining their causes: was it people you met there or just the feeling you experienced? This exercise can reveal hidden aspects of your personality as well as uncover what drives your career decisions or other aspects.

Once you know where you want to head in life, it is easier to assess if you possess the tools or strengths required to reach your life goals. These may include talents, abilities or skills as well as character strengths such as emotional intelligence, resilience and loyalty - and so forth.

Acknowledging one's strengths and abilities builds self-confidence; remaining unaware of them results in lower self-esteem.

To better understand your strengths, keep an ear out for compliments but remain modest when accepting them! For instance, if someone tells you they love your soothing voice, take this as an opportunity to hone this talent and sing more often! In addition, pay attention to any weaknesses so they do not become detrimental to your self-confidence and require remedial action.

Once you become more self-aware and understand yourself (i.e., your personality traits, strengths, weaknesses and triggers), you'll feel empowered knowing you can use that knowledge not only for self-growth but also to gain greater insight into those around you. By knowing yourself better you will know where boundaries need to be drawn as well as which triggers should be avoided so as not to disrupt mental peace - all essential skills for giving 100 percent without feeling exhausted yourself!

Knowledge is power; self-knowledge can bring peace.

Understand Your Biases, Prejudices and Limitations

Chances are, you've heard stories about bias where someone was passed over for employment or targeted by law enforcement due to race, gender or nationality. Our natural perception of such people is that they're bad people for being biased towards certain groups; but most don't realize that researchers in brain and psychological sciences claim that biases and prejudices tend to be subconscious processes which still influence interactions with others and contribute to social injustices in society.

This behavior becomes more obvious when interacting with people outside of your immediate social circle by showing prejudice (emotional biases), discrimination (behavioral biases), and stereotypes (cognitive biases). Such biases may be unconscious (i.e., automatic and ambivalent); they may also have been fostered by society at large; upbringing has an enormous influence. You can develop awareness of your unconscious thinking as well as identify how it influences you from day to day.

How are Biases and Prejudices Formed, and What can be Done About Them?? When considering these questions, one should first focus on where biases and prejudices come from, then on ways of mitigating their effects. Our minds tend to categorize and separate information into separate sections which leads to this behavior. When you form associations in social circumstances by storing, processing, and applying knowledge about others known as Social Cognition; implicit biases arise as our brain searches for patterns to establish connections - something which leads us straight back into implicit biases!

Implicit biases result from our brain's tendency to take shortcuts in an effort to simplify life. Since information overload can make processing data cumbersome and time consuming, mental shortcuts allow us to more quickly sift through it all and find what information pertains.

Although changing other people's biases and prejudices is challenging, by identifying your personal preferences you can help decrease them and help other understand how their prejudices influence their judgment and actions towards others.

Let's start at the foundation. First and foremost, recognize that every person is an individual with individual qualities, strengths and weaknesses that cannot be categorize. Therefore, spend time getting to know people on an intimate level and avoid categorizing or stereotyping people based on stereotypes or prejudice. If your reaction towards someone arises due to one, change your behavior immediately to remove such prejudicial beliefs; although sometimes responses can come fast; take some time after acting to reflect and consider other options before acting in certain ways again.

Change of perspective is also key in shifting one's mentality. By seeing things from other's perspectives, it puts yourself in their shoes and helps you understand where they come from, how they think, and their experiences. Doing this may also instill empathy within you - once this feeling arises, you'll naturally think twice before passing judgment about them.

Engaging with new cultures, ethnicities, and races is also beneficial in broadening your perspective. By giving more time and attention to people from these groups, you will feel an instantaneous sense of belonging that prevents any bias from developing against them.

Apart from yoga and meditation, mindfulness practices such as focused breathing or focused yoga meditation also enable individuals to become self-aware and take control of their thoughts and actions.

Personal biases, prejudices and limitations can be troublesome because they prevent you from seeing people beyond a particular box - which in turn leads to an incorrect understanding of them. But on the positive side, having an open mind and being aware of these restrictions will allow you to work towards eliminating or at least diminishing them - not only will this improve your reading of people but it will broaden your mind further and encourage personal development.

Have you ever found yourself at an impasse, uncertain of which direction to take? After making exhaustive lists of pros and cons for various options available to you, making no headway in making a decision? Each option poses different obstacles, leaving you uncertain how best to move forward.

Under these circumstances, it is important to take an honest inventory of yourself and identify your true desires. But if this process doesn't come naturally to you and pressure has you acting impulsively or complying with people-pleasing behavior instead, the results could be devastating!

Intuition can be your friend in times of trouble. Some call it intuition; others refer to it as their gut feeling or inner voice or hunch; no matter the name it goes by, intuition will guide you along difficult life paths by telling you when the decision aligns with your heart.

However, many people find it challenging to recognize their intuition. That is because our internal hurdles often get in the way, such as overthinking, approval-seeking, should-haves implicit biases and past traumas that prevent us from tapping into it. Overcoming these hurdles requires self-awareness and the capacity to identify what's driving your decisions; when this is achieved strong intuitive thinking ensues leading to decisions that benefit ourselves as individuals and take care in choosing decisions which serve us well.

Well-known people such as Henry Ford are great examples of those who relying on intuition. One such individual was in 1914 when Henry Ford faced declining demand and high turnover at his company. Instead of following conventional advice and increasing employee salaries by 50% he made a bold move and doubled them instead, leading to decreased turnover rates and more workers affording cars for themselves and eventually rising demand again.

Albert Einstein was another notable scientist who disregarded traditional theories of physics due to his intuition. He admitted he believed in inspirations and intuitions and felt confident he was correct despite not knowing for certain. When scientists funded by the Royal Academy conducted experiments testing Einstein's theory of relativity he was certain of their success - no surprise then when an eclipse on May 29, 1919 proved his theory!

Paul McCartney relied heavily on intuition when creating "Yesterday." According to him, he dreamed of writing something that would become immensely popular but was terrified that its contents may differ than expected. Yet still he trusted in himself and relied upon intuition which ultimately lead him towards success and what he considered "the most magical experience."

So what exactly is intuition? One key point about intuition that should be remembered is that it lacks logic; instead it relies on emotional instincts, experiences, or other factors for making decisions. Furthermore, intuition can be divided into three different categories.

* Insight and coherence: This area relates to intelligence (IQ) and involves realizing something without understanding its source.

Subjective intuition refers to having the illusion of knowing something, often used by intellectually curious and puzzle-solving types. * Implicit learning refers to knowing something through picking up cognitive patterns.

Intuition relies on matching up patterns from past experiences with those from present situations, with information processed both consciously and subconsciously by your brain. Your intuition then pulls these thoughts and patterns from your unconscious part of the brain and applies them directly in the current scenario - this leads to decisions being made more swiftly and decisively.

Brain's predictive abilities come into play by matching or mismatching hidden knowledge that has not reached awareness with current experiences.

Why have we turned this into a lecture on intuition? Simply because once you understand its workings and its effect on decision-making, you may be able to differentiate it from fear-induced emotional responses and utilize its insights for making more effective life decisions.

Not only can you identify your intuition, but you can strengthen it further through various exercises.

Deliberate introspection helps increase self-awareness and acknowledge your priorities. Individuals who regularly engage in introspection explore their feelings, where they affect them, and where their emotional responses lie. People who regularly introspect don't fear feeling their emotions; rather they form the habit of asking "How am I feeling about this?" in order to identify and trust their emotions.

Highly intuitive individuals are known for being open and honest with themselves without hiding behind an assumed facade, reflecting upon their needs and wants rather than being trapped by "should-haves." Their perspective is driven by values which helps maintain balance within themselves and keeps intuition under control.

Recharging their energy, they seek solitude from time to time in order to recharge and reflect inwards. Solitude may come in the form of leisurely walks through parks and forests, sipping coffee beside a firepit, or sitting by the sea watching sunset - any activity which allows them to hear their inner voice while giving themselves breathing room.

Empathy is another characteristic commonly found among intuitive people. Their ability to put themselves in other people's shoes and sense how someone else might experience an event makes them the go-to person for many others. Their intuition makes them curious to understand how close ones feel; not out of curiosity but from wanting to establish strong bonds between individuals; the more an intuitive empath becomes acquainted with someone, the easier it becomes for them to predict that person's mood and figure out their needs and emotions. Their senses pick up cues such as body language and social interactions which help them understand more accurately what individuals need from those around them in terms of body language or social interactions which help connect dots so as to understand what each other person needs from them and understanding what people need from others in terms of body language or social interactions which help intuitive empaths sense what each other person needs from them as well.

Intuition can be a powerful resource that can help you escape harmful situations and guide you toward those that will bring greater fulfillment. With its instantaneous responses and mental capacity opening capabilities, intuition helps us make quick, informed decisions. Recognize situations where intuition emerges most readily for you to tap into this resource more fully. Recreate such moments to maximize its power.

Living in today's society shapes our actions, thinking and personalities in many ways; staying true to oneself while navigating this life can be challenging; yet being authentic helps unlock your full potential and realize your fullest potential.

When someone asks you how you're doing, how should you respond? Are you inclined to assume they don't care much and give an insincere answer such as, "I'm fine"? Or should you consider answering honestly how you are actually feeling? Most people choose the latter approach since revealing one's true state will lead to further conversations about themselves that many prefer avoiding.

Idealistically, people would not fear to express themselves freely and wear masks instead of closing off from others. Unfortunately, however, when we keep wearing our masks too long they become difficult to take off, causing us to become someone we aren't and even when alone we begin thinking of how others see us and what others may think about us.

Svend Brinkman, a Danish psychologist, noted that people often expect themselves and others to always appear happy and positive; however, this can have negative side-effects. While being positive can be positive in itself, appearing happy at all times may involve hiding your true feelings so as to please others by appearing positive[14].

No one can remain happy and optimistic all of the time. By pretending everything is fine when you aren't, you stop being assertive and start drifting from who you truly are. Acknowledging negative emotions prompts reflection on what caused it and events which might have contributed to its manifestation; once found, efforts should be made towards solving it; simply keeping problems hidden will only increase their severity over time and become unmanageable.

How can you start on the path towards becoming your true self?

Learn to Be Vulnerable
Being true to yourself means being able to ask for what you need and express it verbally. Expressing feelings through speech allows us to articulate our needs and desires, such as telling someone "it's okay not to be okay". Ignoring one aspect of yourself could mean suppressing another part; being your true self means accepting all parts of you - needy as well as self-sufficient parts alike!

Vulnerability gives others less power to highlight your flaws or weaknesses; once aware, others cannot use these against you.

Take some time to observe how you act when no one is around; what actions please others or yourself? Becoming your authentic, best self does not depend on being successful or having high status; rather it entails developing character through how you behave when no one is present.

To achieve the life you wish for, it is imperative that you are true to who you want to be. Many take an "fake it till you make it" approach in life, but this can become challenging if passion and willingness to live authentically are lacking. A strong character helps develop resilience that allows us to reach our desired destinations more easily.

Character is defined by how you react in any given situation rather than becoming a victim to what happens to you. Doing the right thing when faced with obstacles is part of this concept; another aspect involves making efforts to overcome them in order to prove to others that you can withstand whatever comes your way. Taking charge of your life means being unapologetic with regards to choices and actions made, remaining optimistic even during times of hardship, and becoming your best self in order to create the life you envision for yourself.

But how do you identify what it is you truly desire? Unfortunately, success, status or wealth don't always bring happiness or satisfaction - our desire for materialistic goals comes from not believing that we are enough.

Humans' need to feel "enough" as who they are is what motivates many of them to buy expensive things and dine at luxurious restaurants. Your ego starts telling you to be someone you aren't just to prove your self-worth to others; but this doesn't reflect a true understanding of self-worth.

Ego can suppress our authentic selves with its relentless quest for worth and self-love, so as a means of filling that void we feed it by seeking wealth or status.

Acknowledging that you are enough without all the materialistic frills is key to realizing who you truly are and creating the life you envision for yourself. By believing this deeply within yourself, you can connect with who you really are and shape a fulfilling existence for yourself.

By accepting and acknowledging who you truly are, you send the signal that you're ready to embark on the path set before you by the universe, overcome any challenges in the way, and emerge a happy and content person.

Are We Reading (Judging) Too Hard? A few days ago, while waiting in line to enter my gym for my evening workout session, I overheard two women discussing another gym member who they knew as "fat-a** Judie". One said something like: "I wonder if she is here tonight...".

"Yup, there she is. Jesus, she's such a pea-brain."

When their turn came, both women entered the gym laughing at Judie as entertainment. These were grown women whose source of entertainment lay in criticizing someone dealing with issues in a different way from themselves.

Events such as these serve to remind us that judgment is an unpleasant emotion. Unfortunately, judgment often defines you more than it defines anyone else; yours often stemming from weaknesses within yourself.

Do any of these situations sound familiar to you? "Why does that girl's Instagram have more followers than mine, even though her photos look like they were taken by an elementary student?" What this implies is that you wish your account had more followers, feeling insecure about it all the while.

"That guy always seems happy and nice; it must be fake!" It shows your jealousy of his ability to connect with people and wish that your life were as satisfying that his is; however, rather than working towards improving yourself personally you judge and label others instead.

"He thinks he is so important because of his expensive car and home; how superficial!" Your lips say so, while your heart knows otherwise; however, what your lips express may actually mean that all these luxuries make you wish you were living a different lifestyle, rather than feeling broke constantly.

Look around you and try to identify anyone who seems confident with themselves while harshly judging others. Odds are that there won't be anyone like that because your judgments reveal weaknesses, insecurities and soft spots you attempt to hide from society.

One reason we so easily judge others is because we do the same to ourselves - all roads lead back to "us".

What can you do if you find yourself reading and judging others too harshly? While stopping completely may sound idealistic, that simply isn't possible. However, there is an effective way to catch yourself before turning into an unscrupulous judgment monster: take note when reading or judging someone and stop before becoming one!

Stay curious. Judgment hinders rational thought and prevents you from understanding people or situations; oftentimes these convictions come from limited information.

Curiosity keeps one open to the possibility that there might be more to the situation; something behind-the-scenes you aren't observing.

As soon as someone acts strangely or against your preferences, ask yourself this simple question: "Is there anything happening with that person that I can't see?" This approach may seem obvious but will serve to remind you there's often more going on than meets the eye.

Passing judgment on people can be easy and may even feel satisfying; however, remaining curious requires emotional intelligence, maturity and self-control.

Before making an instantaneous judgment about someone, stop and think before speaking or texting unkind words. Words don't take back, once said they leave an impactful impactful impression that can last a lifetime! Put yourself in their position so you can comprehend their intentions; transform negative thought patterns into constructive ones so you can combat negativity from within - then eliminate its source!

An integral component of personal growth and development is becoming aware of our own flaws, changing patterns to become more positive and mature individuals, while accepting others without judgment or criticism as part of this journey.

As discussed in Part Two, understanding what motivates others is important; but equally essential to your happiness and well-being is identifying and understanding what drives YOU in life. By staying inspired and motivated yourself, you will find energy and drive that can fuel happiness within yourself and spread throughout those around you - much like filling an empty well can't provide relief!

Internal motivation can come from multiple sources, including financial independence, health benefits, stability or self-fulfillment. Every individual is unique in his/her motivation; hence why some thrive more with task or skill-oriented work while others remain with service jobs - these factors determine which path one chooses.

1. Intrinsic Motivation: Activities you enjoy doing for their own sake, like studying crime journalism because watching crime documentaries and reading mystery novels has inspired it.

2. Defined Motivations: Activities you engage in that bring you closer to achieving your goals; for instance, studying crime journalism if your aim is to work as a law enforcement agent.

Studies conducted to explore the effects of intrinsic and identified motivation on children's happiness and well-being showed that those kids who were intrinsically motivated to learn more were psychologically in a better state, regardless of their grades.[15]

Once you understand which motivation drives what actions, the next step should be identifying what drives YOU. Doing a self-evaluation and being honest about how and why you have become who you are now can help identify what drives YOU - then figure out a plan of action to get where you would like to be in life.

Experts advise when trying to identify motivation, it is helpful to recall those moments when you felt most alive and eager about completing something. Reflecting upon those tasks which had an especially high engagement rate may reveal where your passions lie.

Recall those instances and consider what led to your sense of achievement or excitement, then explore their causes by understanding why things happened this way. By answering this question, it can help identify motivators. Here's some questions you can pose to yourself to pinpoint them:

* Who do you envision yourself becoming in two to three years' time?

How would this person behave? If money and resources weren't an issue for you, who would you help out of generosity of spirit? Where would you like to make an impactful statement with regards to what interests or motivates you. * Which hobbies and pursuits make you happy?

* What qualities must you develop to become the best version of yourself and create the life you envision for yourself?

Answer the following questions to uncover your inspirations and lead a life that reflects your values and beliefs.

One important step toward getting motivated is confronting fear. Fear keeps us from progressing forward; it hinders movement, causes us to doubt ourselves at every turn, and leads us down an unnecessary path of caution. Unfortunately, sometimes our fears arise out of imagination rather than an accurate evaluation of risks; even if excitement overshadows fear in order to pursue your task further there will still be parts of ourselves that want to protect from external influences and hold back in an effort to ensure our safety.

To escape this situation, it is necessary to address your fears head on and overcome them. The first step should be recognizing them by speaking aloud; by acknowledging them out loud, their power over you may slowly lessen. Ask yourself these questions:

* What are the chances that what you fear will occur?

And why are you anxious that it might?

By confronting them head on, you can discover which fears are real and which are imagined. Your fears will also indicate where there may be gaps that need filling before reaching your destination and risk management strategies need to be put in place. Once these fears have been dealt with directly, it becomes much simpler to assess what's driving and stopping forward progress faster - knowledge which will allow you to attain your desired goals quicker.

Conversation is an effective and effortless way of building connections, exchanging thoughts, and developing mutual understanding between people. These interactions should be enjoyable and provide insights into individuals' personalities and preferences; through them we develop empathy, feel understood, and hear each other out - creating memorable experiences and lasting growth throughout our lives.

However, to reap these benefits of "conversation," you must reach a point in which people desire conversing with you - this means effortlessly holding attention, commanding the room and shining in social or professional situations.

Are these abilities inherent, or can they be developed through specific training and practice?

Here is the inside information--you can cultivate these abilities by positioning yourself as an interesting, cultured, and knowledgeable individual.

Every human craves being interesting; that is an indisputable truth. Even someone uncomfortable being at the forefront will still want to appear interesting and avoid being labeled a bore! Being interesting leads to influence and opportunities; by understanding what makes an interesting individual tick you could become one yourself and become influential within your circle of influence.

How can you do that?

Begin by being inclusive. Don't try to be "cool" by being dismissive of others - that will only serve to undermine your credibility further. Support people instead of undercutting them: this makes a better impression!

If you see someone at a party or bar holding their drink while searching for someone to talk with, don't ignore them; make an attempt at initiating conversation in order to make them feel seen and included. Perhaps mention something about them that you learned during one of your past conversations; this will show them that you listened when speaking with that individual as well. Establish yourself as a good listener so they perceive you as intriguing.

While being the center of attention is nice, being humble is also essential. Studies show that people enjoy spending time around those who exhibit humility. Since this term can vary considerably depending on context, let's use as our definition: respecting other's opinions and perspectives as being humble - this will show someone they matter!

Be careful not to confuse humility with lack of self-respect or assertiveness; being humble does not require self-deprecating behavior that makes someone else feel special. Be humble by acknowledging your abilities and what they can or cannot do; even something as simple as saying, "I don't know the answer yet but will research and get back to you," or admitting "I'm unfamiliar with this topic; can you tell me more?" can show humility.

Avoid being intimidated by showing that you have an open, beginner's mind! Another effective strategy for driving conversations forward is being genuine generosity, as this provokes a psychological response of reciprocity from others. We don't mean materialistic gestures such as buying gifts or food; simply have open conversations, give compliments freely or ask someone how they're feeling without asking just out of formality!

By being generous with your time and attention, you will discover that others become more interested in you. They will appreciate knowing you're not there just to gain material benefits from their presence.

Be generous by saying "yes." If you possess specific expertise or insights regarding an area of concern for others, use them freely without considering what will come back in return.

Being interesting and helpful will enable you to earn favor among others and establish life-long relationships. By following the conversation practices mentioned here, it will become easy to become the topic of conversation interest.

Have You Experienced Long Pauses and Awkward Looks, Which Have Made Conversation Uncomfortable

Everyone at some point will experience long pauses and awkward looks during conversations that makes us uncomfortable, which is when we realize the importance of keeping the dialogue going; also known as keeping people invested in their discussions.

Here is how you can do that-Find a common interest. People vary greatly with regards to interests and priorities; finding something in common helps build bridges between you. Once you find something similar between two people, jot down everything you find interesting about it (as conversation starters). Go over that list several times so it sticks in your memory easily when conversation points arise in that area - then refer back to it when necessary! Additionally, write down conversation starters about topics relevant to both of you so there will never be an end to discussion!

Interesting topics include football, the latest gadget introduced into the market, watching a movie or reading a book you found enjoyable or hearing comments by Donald Trump that made you laugh out loud.

Don't be shy to pose open-ended questions when you find yourself at a loss for words - an open-ended inquiry requires more than an "yes/no" response and is sure to spark conversation between parties involved.

Example topics might include: A Concert: My Thoughts
What Movie Scene did You Enjoy Most and Going out Alone or Groups?

These questions encourage people to open up more about themselves. By eliminating awkward silences between conversations, these types of questions keep dialogue flowing more effortlessly between you and another individual.

By asking these kinds of questions, you are showing someone that you care about their opinions and emotions - this builds relationships by keeping the dialogue going between yourself and them. They'll appreciate this effort you put forth to maintain it!

Establish Emotional Bonds

Conversations should not simply be seen as words: they serve to build emotional connections between people. While you could carry out an entire dialogue without sharing meaningful information, doing so helps establish meaningful bonds and gives an inside glimpse of another's personality.

Blurt! When nothing else works, don't hesitate to speak up! Conversation can often become challenging because we fear our words might be boring for others; therefore, our thoughts and words remain hidden until our fears of being judged manifest themselves into words or action. But oftentimes this fear stems from nothing more than imagination!

Next time you find yourself in such an encounter, speak your mind freely (so long as it doesn't contain racist or sexually offensive material). You may be amazed to find out that people aren't as narrow-minded as you imagined!

Your efforts at continuing a conversation will only succeed if both participants are invested in it and willing to engage fully. If they show signs of disinterest or refuse to contribute at all, take that as an indicator that it should end immediately.

No Matter Your Interests Or Goals It is undeniable that personal relationships are key to personal and professional success, regardless of one's interests, personal goals or profession. Yet you may have noticed that some individuals seem able to connect easily with all they meet while others struggle even to have healthy conversations let alone develop meaningful relationships with them.

Here is how you can approach and get the attention of beautiful girls at a bar, the department head at an annual event or your next-door neighbor by signing a petition for making the neighborhood safe.

So how can you develop this skill?

First and foremost, remember that people respond better to genuine people. Making and keeping connections begins with genuine intentions; any attempt at superficial interactions will only last so long. Talking with people just for promotions or free tickets won't cut it - if you truly care about people they can become genuine friends over time.

Two, demonstrate your willingness to give someone you are trying to connect with the time and attention. Sometimes due to limited resources, we may not be able to shower people with gifts or materialistic displays of affection; giving someone genuine time learning about their preferences and likes is just as impactful a gesture in showing they matter.

If you are having difficulty learning more about them through independent research, connecting with people they know could help immensely. People tend to mimic our habits and hobbies so by knowing people they like more intimately you may gain some insights into them as well.

Making connections can also be invaluable in professional settings; many job vacancies are filled through referrals and networking; thus by creating relationships, you open yourself up to endless opportunities.

When someone recommends you for a job, their recommendation can vouch for your credibility, making it easier to secure that job. Don't underestimate building relationships with colleagues simply because you spend limited time together; more people in your social circle means more opportunities in life!

Once you've established a connection, the next step should be fostering it and keeping it strong. Unfortunately, once someone is out of sight they oftentimes fall from people's memories; to make sure you stay unforgettable the easiest way is with small gestures like sending Christmas cards, birthday messages through text messaging or their favorite book with a personal note - you might be amazed how pleased people will be by these reminders that show they matter! We all crave being remembered; show someone they matter by showing that your relationship values them! You could just create lifelong connections!

All it takes to win over people is showing that you understand and value them; then you will gain their loyalty.

T he digital age has made it easier than ever for us to automate tasks and use machines to manage our workload, yet the more tech we rely upon, the farther away from experiencing the emotions involved with completing a task or overcoming difficulties to complete our work is felt.

Emotional intelligence comes into play here; it refers to your ability to recognize both your own emotions as well as those around you, including how these affect others and affect their thoughts and behavior. By comprehending human feelings more deeply, emotionally intelligent people find it easier to connect with other people while being more compassionate and understanding towards those they encounter; this quality contributes greatly to their professional and personal success.

People often get confused between emotional intelligence and intelligence quotient (IQ), given they both represent different forms of intelligence. The main distinction lies in how each is measured and represented.

IQ measures mental intelligence through standardised tests and is directly tied to mental capabilities; for example, being able to comprehend information and apply it in solving problems. People with higher IQ are adept at making fast mental connections and catering abstract ideas quickly. Emotional intelligence refers to how one uses emotions in order to make sense of situations; those at the higher end of this scale tend to be emotionally stable individuals able to manage their feelings well while dealing with those going through hard phases effectively.

Another difference between these two forms of intelligence is that IQ is something you inherit at birth while emotional intelligence develops from experiences during your upbringing and surrounding. You can work to become emotionally intelligent as an adult by cultivating strong people skills.

Here's how you can accomplish that:

* Be mindful of your reactions. Don't jump to judgment before fully understanding all aspects of a situation, instead try seeing things from others' points of view and keep an open mind without succumbing to stereotypes or biases. By being accepting of others' viewpoints and accepting their opinion(s), you build their trust.

* Assess yourself. Are you aware of your weaknesses? Can you accept that working on some areas of yourself in order to become a better person is needed? Take an honest and thoughtful look at yourself and be brave enough to change those parts that impede growth - it could transform your life! * Take an honest and thoughtful look at yourself! Being honest can be life-altering!

* Evaluate how you respond in stressful situations. How do you deal with disappointments when things don't go as expected, for example when things don't work out? Do you lash out or blame others instead? Being able to manage disappointments

calmly is extremely valuable in both professional and personal settings - it prevents emotional outbursts from leading to hasty decisions or actions you might regret later on.

* Don't seek validation of your accomplishments. Humility can be an invaluable emotional toolbox asset; practicing it shows others you recognize your own strengths and achievements without needing to boast about them to others. Instead, focus on others' accomplishments as a way of inspiring yourself! You may just see that their achievements rub off on you.

* Take responsibility for your actions. If you cause offense to another, apologize or attempt to resolve the situation immediately if needed. Don't ignore their feelings or gaslight them into believing they shouldn't have been hurt in any way; by showing an effort towards rectifying things honestly and making amends you demonstrate to that individual that they are valued by you and that everything possible will be done to maintain relationships between both of you.

* Be mindful of the effects of your actions. Before undertaking any course of action, always take into account how it will impact those involved in the situation and their reactions to what you propose doing. Would it harm them or exacerbate matters further for them? If this is the case, avoid going forward with it altogether; but if that cannot be avoided for some reason, ensure to discuss this decision with them first and try to find ways to minimize its adverse consequences.

Emotional intelligence is key for reading and comprehending people. It allows you to form strong bonds with individuals, which ultimately leads to success in all aspects of your life.

When your partner comes home after a hard day at work, do they think to themselves: "Finally! I can relax now!" or do they think instead: "Here it comes again!" If you want a successful marriage or relationship, you would ideally like for them to think the former phrase - even though coming home to an immaculate home may be nice, what matters more is having them feel at ease in an environment they enjoy staying in and feel welcomed and welcome by you as much as the cleanliness factor itself.

What should you do when you have had a rough day? Smile and try to be nice as with strangers in a meeting, or dump all your emotional scraps onto them? Strange how those closest to us often see our worst side. One may argue that without being "real" with each other in our homes and relationships, who else would we open up to? But can you handle all the frequent fuming and fussing from them too?

Therefore, it's essential that you do not create an environment you won't be able to live in yourself. Sure, everyone has moments where anxiety, anger or stress take control. However, make an effort to limit these incidents so your partner does not come home to negativity. If these emotions seem hard for you to manage alone, talk with friends or therapists for support; only when your mental health is stable can you create an optimal atmosphere for both of you.

Attracting your partner requires keeping technology out of the equation when speaking with them; give your full attention without scrolling through your Twitter feed simultaneously; listen to how their day went and report back what you did during it; if your home is large enough, keep laptops or computers out of sight so as to reduce temptation to check in too often; decluttering will allow for frequent reconnections instead of just one date night each week.

Additionally, external influences can help create an ideal atmosphere. For instance, make sure both you and your home smell nice when your partner arrives - this will instantly refresh them mentally while making them feel closer. Light scented candles and play light music to set a romantic, cozy ambiance; your companion is sure to want to stay with you longer!

Your home should be an oasis of comfort and peace - if you can help build one together with your partner, that will go a long way toward having a successful partnership.

Acknowledging their Comfort Zones and Accommodating Them

Does your relationship involve sweatpants, farts in bed, and your partner yelling "Babe, that pimple can take over your entire face!"? If this describes the dynamic between you and your partner, then you have successfully established an enjoyable connection that is built to last.

At some point in your relationship, you may encounter situations in which an activity or social situation you wanted to engage in was beyond the comfort zone of your partner.

To maintain peace in the relationship and avoid disagreement, it's essential that both partners understand where their comfort levels end and how far you can push them to move out of them.

If you are an extrovert and your partner is an introvert, they might not enjoy attending as many parties and outdoor activities as you do. Therefore, finding an acceptable compromise where neither partner feels constrained by staying indoors too much; and where neither feels overexposed due to constant social interactions is key for finding happiness together.

To accommodate their preferences, start by understanding their moods - such as when they feel like going out versus when they want to spend more time at home with Netflix and books. Also try not going out consecutive days and allow for their energy reserves to recharge themselves before going back out again. These small adjustments in your attitude will show them that you care for their preferences while encouraging them to go beyond their comfort zones to accommodate you too!

Studies have demonstrated that when couples feel at ease in their companionship relationships, the odds of them lasting longer increase significantly. Conversely, reaching a comfort level means less excitement or new experiences to explore and risks becoming stale over time. So, how can you balance accommodating both of your partners comfort levels while keeping the romance alive?

Try surprising each other on occasion - not with something as big as buying a new car without consulting your partner first - instead, focus on smaller, meaningful gestures such as providing their favorite meal when returning from work, wearing your sexiest lingerie to bed, or planning surprise dates to show your love how thoughtful you are. These small surprises will add the element of surprise without going too far outside their comfort zones.

Couples who become too comfortable can easily fall into the no-talking zone, expecting that their partner can read them without them having to say anything themselves. But reality can often prove otherwise!

Understanding yourself may come easily to others based on patterns and predictable behaviors, but sometimes they simply cannot meet your expectations. When this occurs, communication and voicing your feelings become paramount; don't suppress feelings when they arise; express them openly instead! If something has hurt you deeply or emotionally if they need someone to sit with or hold their hand just let them know! A heart-to-heart is always the most effective way of connecting with those closest to us.

If expressing their emotions isn't something your partner feels comfortable doing, accommodate them by learning their non-verbal cues and don't push too hard for them to express themselves. Over time, you will notice their appreciation of you letting them stay within their comfort zone.

Your partner's comfort zone is the space where they allow you to truly see them for who they truly are--both their strengths and their flaws. By learning to stay with them in this zone, you will discover their personality more readily and learn to interpret it easily.

Being Vulnerable

We have spoken extensively about vulnerability throughout this book and it bears repeating that emotional exposure provides you with strength to open yourself up to experiences and love. Many are afraid of showing their vulnerability because they think it makes them look weak - this simply isn't true! Here's why.

By sharing your true self with those closest to you, you show your courage in being seen for who you truly are and being seen for who you truly are - creating a sense of belonging, love and authenticity in relationships that matter most.

Stepping forward with courage to be vulnerable has many emotional advantages. By placing yourself in situations that make you vulnerable, such as placing yourself in situations that test your mettle and test out how capable you are of managing challenging scenarios - building self-confidence while strengthening resilience against obstacles along the way.

Showing vulnerability with friends, partners and parents can foster empathy. Doing so allows them to witness your soft spots that you tend to keep hidden from others - telling them that they matter more than everyone else by opening this side up to them.

Beyond improving relationships with others, empathy also strengthens your connection with yourself. By accepting undesirable or weak aspects of yourself and accepting those as part of who you are, empathy increases self-acceptance and thus contributes to overall wellness.

Following are a few suggestions to help you become vulnerable: * Be open to taking chances that may result in rejection. Communicate honestly about what you want out of relationships - specifically your expectations and boundaries - along with personal topics you typically don't discuss with anyone else, like personal matters that come up in conversation and discussing past mistakes made in relationships.

* Discuss incidents that evoke feelings of fear, shame or grief.

So far we've explored just a few ways in which accepting vulnerability helps one grow; it opens doors for change while building flexibility.

Change can be daunting for many because it involves leaving their comfort zone and venturing into unknown territory. Therefore, this process requires extensive work - the first step being learning to be vulnerable. Imagine you're trying to break an indefinable bad habit like excessive eating, which has negatively impacted your health, looks and budget. In order to do that successfully, however, you first must identify its root cause; what's driving you toward food in the first place? Are You Eating to Escape Emotions, Stress or Anxiety, or Out of Boredness? In order to overcome your addiction to food, an honest look into yourself must take place - acknowledging your dark habits will not change overnight, just like how their feelings cannot.

Change requires honest, no-deflective self-analysis - and vulnerability is the gateway to it all!

Vulnerability can open your mind to new perspectives. The key to welcoming diverse viewpoints and ideas lies in accepting that your experiences were not all-consuming in life; temporarily giving up beliefs and values for other points of view can be challenging; yet vulnerability helps you see there's more beyond yourself, as you come to recognize there are people living outside your desires and needs as well as accepting all perspectives equally in order to form meaningful connections with those people living there.

There's an age-old adage: everything you put out into the world comes back to you in some form or another. That applies equally well when it comes to relationships or connections - what you bring will reflect back onto you in kind; for instance, love, empathy, tolerance and patience will pay dividends in form of strong and meaningful connections, while vice versa.

Now that you understand how people work, it is time to put all that knowledge to use! In this section, we will put all your learning to good use - deciphering even the most carefully kept secrets can be tricky; here, we will explore what gives people away, spotting lies quickly, and breaking through any barriers people often set up against themselves.

People reading is all about paying attention to the small details and observations that often slip by unnoticed. As an experienced people reader, you cannot allow even small differences such as nose flicking or nail twitches to go unnoticed; therefore this section aims to teach you how to identify these micro details that help make accurate assessments.

Have you ever observed what someone looks like when they're lying? Unfortunately, there is no single answer as every individual displays different indicators of lying. Body language, facial expressions, choice of words and habits may give away whether someone is lying. Verbal and nonverbal cues such as these can help identify lies versus truth - though you might not recognize the term baseline itself!

Baselining people gives you the power to evaluate individuals on their truthfulness. By providing an objective measure against which to compare and judge whether their behavior is out of character, or simply indicative of them acting normally.

So how can you identify baseline behaviors? Here are three easy steps that will help you do just that!

Step 1: Start with the handshake.

As they say, first impressions last and you only get one chance at making that initial impactful statement about someone. Also consider this the ideal moment to assess a person's actions since most are at their most positive during an initial meeting.

Salespeople and interviewers are adept at using this skill, often creating a favorable first impression with customers or potential hires after just one handshake. Their secret? Paying close attention to gaze, vocal quality and posture when greeting newcomers with an introduction handshake.

No matter whether in a social or professional situation, keeping tabs on people's social cues and taking mental notes will allow you to assess them more quickly. Even though this might feel intrusive at times, know that all this data is subconsciously coming into our minds anyway; by making a conscious effort to remember its presence we can quickly make connections in terms of behavior.

When shaking someone's hand, pay attention to how they make small talk, tell jokes, and respond to personal questions in a natural setting. This information can help establish a baseline.

Step 2: Stimulate Different Reactions by Posing Questions.

The key to creating an accurate baseline is gathering an individual's normal reactions in different situations - how they react when happy, sad or bored are just examples - although this may be difficult in everyday settings such as funerals - though sometimes asking specific questions to gauge reactions could provide insights into them more closely.

Do David or Jane show signs of discomfort when you tell them "no"? Does Kevin raise his eyebrows when speaking with Taylor?

Your reactions in non-threatening circumstances will provide the basis of how this person reacts in more dangerous scenarios.

Eye movement can be used as an indicator of deviation from normal behavior. According to researchers worldwide, those engaging in dishonest activities usually maintain eye contact when speaking, though their pattern differs from normal conditions - for instance they might look down or glance elsewhere while speaking; or exhibit constant eye contact at first but then switch after trigger questions or stressors cause it to change suddenly; similarly blinking slower or faster than usual may also signal something suspicious is going on.

Other aspects to keep an eye out for when conducting baselines include seated and standing postures, vocal speed and tone, laughter style, nervous tics, hand gestures and expressions of excitement and surprise. What many don't realize is that their face often betrays true emotions with microexpressions like brief cracks of smile or lifting of eyebrows that happen for only milliseconds but reveal exactly how a person truly feels - unlike body language which can be controlled in part through awareness of it.

Professionals agree that emotions exhibited during facial tells don't always indicate guilt; sometimes they simply don't want to express what's on their minds. When someone exhibits these symptoms, probe further by asking specific questions as to why they are feeling this way.

Step 3: Keep a mental record of baseline behavior.

The final key to solving this puzzle lies in remembering everything you observe mentally. File away their behavior along with any additional info like spouse, profession or hometown address if necessary - especially if your memory is weak! Providing this extra detail may help connect dots more quickly while recalling other details more readily; just don't write everything down, let your brain remember!

Have you ever attended a party where, while recounting an engaging story from work to a group of people, all that was heard in response was, "Oh yeah! Great. Are they serving shrimps?" and your energy quickly dissipated as quickly wrapped your story to wrap up, without feeling satisfied about how things had turned out?

What happened was someone was only half listening and asked an irrelevant question that killed both your dialogue and mood. To keep a conversation flowing smoothly, pay attention and pose relevant queries - this will get them talking more freely and ultimately enable you to gain a deeper insight into them, helping you read them better in return. It's like the domino effect!

Invitation is one of the fundamental tools of communication; it informs those present that it's their turn to speak while offering suggestions about topics they could explore.

Example: Asking, "How was the last book you read?" opens up an invitation for conversation regarding that specific topic you addressed in your question.

These invitations serve as an essential safety net when conversation drifts off-track. If you find yourself struggling to come up with topics for conversation, try throwing an invite into the mix - especially if it relates to something you've discussed previously! Otherwise it won't do any harm initiating new topics altogether.

Invitations can take the form of questions or statements. When using question-based invitations, be sure to keep the language open-minded and relatable for maximum response.

These open-ended questions allow the person in front of you to elaborate instead of providing short replies. For instance, asking, "Did you have a good trip?" will likely result in either yes or no answers. By contrast, asking "How was your trip?" you may receive more detailed replies that show the other person you care and motivate them to share more details of their trip with you.

By taking an interest in getting to know another, you demonstrate your own. This creates an empowering bond between you and that individual and allows them to open up more.

Similar to asking insightful questions, asking insightful questions of them shows your interest. Following the classic rule "show, don't tell," by asking perceptive questions you show people you care - though be wary of being nosy!

Next comes our task of asking good and insightful questions.

Doing the latter won't give you much insight into their true selves, as even they won't understand why you are interested. They might assume you care more about the weather than them! Likewise, by asking intimate questions such as "What is your deepest darkest desire?," you could make them uncomfortable and want to escape from you as quickly as possible.

Start out small and intuitive. As your questions progress, gradually ask more intimate ones while considering the comfort level of the other person. If at any point they appear bothered by your inquiries or displaying signs of discomfort, stop. Instead, switch back to less intrusive questions until given permission to continue probing deeper.

Before delving too deeply into someone's personality, however, two important considerations should be kept in mind.

First and foremost, transitioning a relationship from formal to intimate does not happen overnight; rather it's a gradual process which takes several conversations over time. At first conversations may revolve around surface-level topics like family and hobbies; over time these could expand to personal discussions such as past relationships or childhood trauma.

Remind yourself that every conversation offers the chance to build rapport and gain more insight into a person. Over time, they may feel more at ease sharing personal details about themselves.

Second, establish trust. If you ask someone to divulge intimate details of their life, be prepared to do the same in return. Sharing details about yourself will open a channel of trust between the two of you that can build confidence within any relationship.

Invitation questions are great at opening up dialogue, but they won't do the job alone. So use follow-up queries to extend the dialogue.

Put simply, asking someone questions like, "How are you feeling about it?" or "Why did you say that?" shows genuine curiosity for their story or message and provides them with validation that their thoughts are valued by someone. This also gives you the chance to demonstrate value as you listen intently during conversations that might otherwise seem too uncomfortable or boring for you.

Next time someone talks in vague terms, instead of just nodding and moving along quickly, ask them, "What did you mean by that?" To extend and make more meaningful conversations here are some additional ideas:

* What are you up to these days, your sister/brother/spouse? * How did your day go - and what was its most exciting part? * Why did you make such a thoughtful remark? * Could you elaborate and help me understand it further?

* Do you believe your thoughts would change on this issue and eventually change their minds about it?

Before answering each question, allow the other person time and space to respond, without interrupting during their response. Listening is key when getting to know someone better!

Einstein famously advised, "Question Everything". Asking insightful questions of those we interact with helps create efficient interactions, build trust relationships and form meaningful bonds.

How often have you thought, "I've had enough. They always lie!"? Whether after a failed relationship or job promotion promise gone astray, lying is always disappointing and can leave us questioning our judgment and trusting in people we once trusted less and less. What if there's a way out? This chapter will equip you with tools for becoming your own human lie detector so that you can recognize any suspicious signs quickly and learn to trust only reliable individuals.

Truth be told, most people occasionally lie. Sometimes it may just be tiny white lies like "No honey, that dress doesn't make you look fat!" but in other instances lies can be more obvious like, "My mother was sick so that's why I was late today", or outright deceptive like, "I'm not having an affair; I had another all-nighter at work".

However, most people are poor at recognizing lies, leading them to be deceived. A study conducted to examine this area showed that only 54% of participants could detect falsehoods correctly.[16]

Behavior differences between individuals who lie and those who tell the truth can be difficult to assess, since there are no distinct telltale signs that would allow one to identify either group; however, subtle indicators may help distinguish one from the other. As mentioned previously in another chapter, variations from baseline behavior is another indicator of lying.

However, it's essential to recognize that lie detection relies heavily on trusting your gut. By knowing what signs to look out for and learning how to interpret them with your knowledge and instincts, lie detection will become much simpler for you.

Psychologists and researchers across multiple industries have conducted extensive studies on deception and body language in order to help law enforcement members detect fraudsters and liars more quickly and accurately. The result of this research has highlighted several potential red flags which might indicate any deceit:

* Being deliberately vague by volunteering minimal details; Being unable to provide specifics about any event or incident

Repeating sentences or questions when answering specific queries; Talking in sentence fragments.

* Exhibiting grooming behaviors such as pressing fingers to lips or manipulating hair strands

As is true with anything else, practice makes perfect in lie detection as well. Reading research and learning tells can only get you so far; to truly master lie detection requires paying close attention and being 100% aware.

As such, we now turn our focus to indicators or signs you should look out for when trying to spot an impostor.

First and foremost, be aware of what signals to watch out for. While people rely on valid cues to detect lies, their reliability as lie indicators could be limited. Some common deception cues that people observe include:

* Exhibiting Indifference: When someone attempts to remain emotionally neutral by suppressing expression and showing no tells, they might show a lack of expression, assume an impassive posture or shrug as ways of not divulging too much information.

* Vocal Incoherence: If a speaker seems uncertain of themselves and starts mumbling or stammering while speaking, this could be because their brain cannot think fast enough to cover their lies.

* Overthinking: When someone seems intent on distorting the truth, overthinking can often be the result. With proper knowledge of what signs to look out for and an ability to use judgment effectively in any given situation, understanding can become much simpler.

Second, don't rely solely on body language. Most lie detection books and blogs advocate focusing solely on body language--the subtle changes in behavior and physical signs that reveal who's being dishonest--to catch deceivers. However, research now indicates that body language cues may help spot lies but are not always reliable indicators of deception.

Howard Ehrlichman, a research psychologist, found that changes in eye movements did not always indicate lying; they could simply be caused by retrieving information from long-term memory or thinking too hard.[17]

From these and other studies, it can be concluded that body language, while often accurate, may not always be the best indicator of lying. Knowing someone and their behavior patterns gives an edge in distinguishing lying from baseline behavior patterns.

Thirdly, ask them to narrate their story - backwards! The theory behind this exercise is that nonverbal and verbal cues that distinguish truth from lies become more prominent when cognitive load increases - this is because lying is an exhausting process compared to telling the truth - hence why people say "if you tell the truth, you don't have to remember all of its details".

Deliberate lies are more cognitively challenging activities; those engaging in them require a great deal of mental resources in trying to conceal any tells that might give away their lies, monitoring both their own behavior and that of listeners. Establishing credibility and convincing others of their story takes effort, but when combined with the demand to narrate it backward, you may begin spotting any cracks in their narrative or behavior discrepancies. Research has substantiated this theory. If a story appears thin on details, or is completely made-up, remember what details were repeated the first time! Doing this will allow you to distinguish between lies and truth.

As previously discussed, trust your instincts! As previously indicated, following your gut may be your greatest weapon against lie detection. Numerous studies have proven that internal subconscious indicators are more effective than conscious strategies in detecting deception. Humans possess intuitive, unconscious data which aid in recognizing deceit if we pay attention to it.

Though instincts can be highly reliable, people often lack the skill or ability to accurately use them and remain vulnerable to deceitful thinking. Unfortunately, however, conscious thought or reaction may interfere with automatic associations - instead of trusting your gut instinct, your conscious thoughts start analyzing patterns or stereotypical actions and eventually talk yourself out of trusting it altogether. Knowing yourself well enough allows you to recognize instinctive responses while not overemphasizing behaviors which lead down the road towards self-doubt and make you questioning whether it could work on occasion!

Finally, observe their confidence level change. Paying attention will show you that a potential deceiver's style changes when they are confronted; most liars feel secure within their limited zone of lying, where they feel in control; however if anything challenges anything they say it may cause them to lose control and thus lower confidence levels significantly.

As they begin to feel pressured, you may notice them altering their narrative or providing inconsistent answers about certain events, becoming more erratic in their answers and changing how they describe them. By watching for behavioral changes like this you may spot gaps in their story and identify their true intentions.

Be mindful that it may be hard to determine whether someone in front of you is telling the truth or making up stories; perhaps they are adept at concealing information, or your trust may make it hard for you to spot anything amiss. But the signs and indicators outlined above may give away that someone is hiding something from you.

Next time you need to assess someone's honesty, pay close attention to any subtle clues linked to lies. If necessary, increase pressure by making it rationally taxing for them to tell their tale. By keeping these practices in place and keeping these tips at heart, you will be able to quickly reduce those who are being dishonest with you from your life.

How Can You Tell If Someone Is Lying by Omission? How Can You Determine Whether Someone Is Lying by Omission? If someone doesn't explicitly lie but instead presents only part of the truth, is this considered lying or simply communicating? Lying by omission is a clever tactic used to avoid telling everything that happened; for the purposes of record it should be considered lying as it prevents its receiver from getting an accurate understanding. For example, a child might tell you they put ice cream in the freezer only then later come out later and eat it all themselves; for record this should be classified as lying, since it prevents the receiver of information from seeing all sides. For instance a kid might say they put ice cream in the freezer but then fail to mention they took it out later from where it had come out later as opposed to telling them fully of all facts such as taking it out later and eating it later when asked by you as possible.

However, their answer did not provide you with enough detail if your question was "Where did the ice cream go?"; regardless of how accurate their story may have been.

Problematic with lying with omission lies is that most individuals using it don't consider it to be lying, therefore not being as reluctant or showing typical signs of someone telling a falsehood. To fully comprehend why someone lies, we need to know their motivation; people may withhold important information due to shame, guilt or fear but since they're reluctant to tell full-on lies it might be easier for investigators to get at the truth if someone leaves important details out in conversations.

Scan for signs that someone seems uncomfortable when discussing an important subject. Do they sound vague, take too many breaks, avoid eye contact? Ask specific questions for clarity to force people to make conscious decisions about whether or not to share specific details, no longer being able to hide behind "I'm not lying", allowing you to learn the whole truth more readily than when someone lies freely without hesitation. Even if someone lies, their signs will likely be easier to detect compared with someone who repeatedly lies without hesitation.

Have you ever met someone that immediately made you uneasy, yet couldn't identify why they seemed uncomfortable to you? Did something seem wrong in their way of looking at you but couldn't pinpoint what exactly? Have they made you uncomfortable but you couldn't put your finger on why they looked that way? If this sounds familiar to you then Chapter 22 may provide the solution: Acquiring Accuracy When Thin Slicing.

"Something didn't feel quite right." You would find yourself trying in vain to explain to your spouse why you had not selected that specific dentist for dental procedures or why you declined an impressive job offer.

Everyday we come into contact with various people; some we barely know and others that leave lasting impressions. You might recall someone you briefly met at a park as warm or kind while another stranger may stand out as rude or weird.

Are all our initial judgments unjustified and due to our own prejudices? Maybe not! Perhaps first impressions matter because they reveal something about someone that our conscious minds simply can't comprehend yet. This ability of making quick yet accurate assumptions about people quickly is known as thin slicing.

First impressions or judgments about someone's personality don't happen by chance alone - they are actually created by our subconscious minds processing information much faster than we realize! Why can some of us make better judgments than others, you ask?

What sets apart those making accurate judgments from those who don't is their trust of their "intuition." They listen to what their gut tells them and develop these skills through conscious effort.

Thin slicing can be defined scientifically as the ability to make informed judgments based on small bits of information. Multiple experiments have proven that our conclusions about someone are consistent regardless of how long we converse with them - from five seconds or five minutes![18] Our subconscious observes subtler traits about them like blinking eyelids, stiff postures, smiles or gestures which tend to slip past us without our conscious minds noticing.

Can't that be amazing? To accurately make assumptions about someone based on just a statement or micro trait could be so accurate.

So why haven't we been adept at mind reading people so far? Mostly due to being unable to articulate these judgments. Not having enough details at our fingertips means this nonverbal decoding takes place without us even realizing it, thus giving first impressions so much importance despite them not reflecting reality but instead acting as signals from our subconscious minds that they may hold answers for us.

As humans, we're wired to trust only ourselves within limits. Negative bias prevents us from trusting ourselves too strongly. You might be thinking to yourself: 'All this sounds great; however if I had trusted my gut more completely I wouldn't have purchased this book!"

I understand your dilemma; trusting my gut too often led me down a road of gambling losses! And while I don't advocate letting your subconscious mind guide your judgments, our brains are much smarter than we give them credit for! Did you know our brains can process 11 million bits of information every second? Yet our conscious minds only seem capable of processing 40-50 bits. [19] That's an enormous gap between what our brain can actually handle and what we perceive it can handle; while we may only be processing a meager 50 bits, our subconscious brain has already observed, deduced, and formed opinions far more accurate than anything our conscious awareness could ever provide us.

Comparatively speaking, our subconscious has done an outstanding job processing information; unfortunately we just don't recognize its efforts enough. Imagine if we trusted our subconscious more in making judgements; no other skill may be needed to access people's brains!

Discovering the art of thin slicing requires us to recognize our subconscious thoughts and interpret our intuition correctly. Don't bury those little judgments that might slip by unnoticed. When labeling someone, ask yourself why and think harder: was it their shifting weight from leg to leg or did they bite their lip just before speaking out?

As powerful as our subconscious is, it can also collide with conscious biases and lead to some unfortunate decisions. Therefore, not everyone relies solely on their gut when making decisions - the potential power lies within us all, it just needs unlocking and tapping properly.

Thin slicing involves learning more about someone with minimal information. Their mannerisms, body language, handwriting and clothing all reveal much about them if only observed carefully and aware of one's subconscious. According to Malcolm Gladwell's best-selling book Blink, thin slicing involves tapping into one's "adaptive subconscious." While conscious minds use evidence-based assessments when drawing their conclusions about people or events based on conscious observation alone, adaptive unconscious uses assessments with very small chunks of evidence at best as its sources.

As we practice and perfect this craft of thin slicing information, our success depends on being able to practice and learn with every experience we gain. By tapping into your subconscious and filtering information instead of assessments, you can better understand others and predict their behavior.

John Gottman, an esteemed American psychologist, conducted an in-depth research study involving over 3,000 couples to develop what has come to be known as the "love lab." Through this method of information gathering and disaggregation, Gottman concluded that you could predict the future of marriage by thinly slicing relevant data - not only gathering it all together but understanding its relevance too. This theory focused on not simply gathering facts but determining what information was most pertinent.

And that is precisely what you should be doing too. Your subconscious will be receiving millions of bits of data, but your conscious mind must now decide what information is important or irrelevant; herein lies the value of knowledge provided in other parts of the book; use its tools to discern which actions, words and indicators need your focus and which aren't pertinent in terms of understanding people better.

Gottman's theory suggests focusing on fleeting facial expressions and dialogues that appear trivial, without drawing too much attention to themselves. While it won't yield results immediately, practice is required in recognizing patterns - you need to identify people who lie, guard their emotions well or conceal behind extrovert behaviors - so as time progresses your conscious and subconscious minds will align seamlessly and allow for calculated assessments of what lies within someone's mind. [23]

At times we all find ourselves trying to decipher what someone means when they use phrases such as "I don't care" or "Why do you think it matters" or "I am fine"; these can feel like ticking bombs that require you to quickly figure out their true intent before any lasting damage is done to relationships! You find yourself wishing that years ago you had signed up for that telepathy workshop!

An interpretation can often be hard, especially when they don't use words to communicate their ideas directly. Words are only part of the picture - in order to save the ship, one must get to the bottom of the ocean to locate where monsters lurk - this is what reading between the lines is all about!

Reading between the lines is an art that can save even the closest relationships. It requires understanding which leaves little room for explanations and allows you to create the ideal environment for meaningful and productive dialogues. Meaning often lies beyond words alone - which is why full stops, commas, and exclamation marks play such an essential role in communicating their meaning.

Signs that people give off to reveal their true emotions can often be misread as innocent gestures; but these signs should always be taken seriously as indicators that what people say has an underlying meaning; for instance, words like "I want to always be with you" could seem like a declaration of love but when combined with other red flags in an uncertain relationship could indicate abuse or manipulation.

As one can expect in an environment inhabited by over 8 billion individuals with their individual thoughts and personalities, one sentence might not mean the same when spoken by different people in various contexts. You must listen harder in order to comprehend what another person is trying to convey. According to Gary Wong, an esteemed real estate investor and coach, we have two ears but only one mouth, so listening should take precedence over speaking[23]. Be open-minded towards what people are telling you while understanding deeply what their intentions are when speaking their language.

One effective strategy to help you read between the lines is waiting a moment before speaking out. Rushing to reply can mean missing out on taking time to understand what was actually said; and if your counterpart does the same, their message could easily get lost among misunderstanding and poor communication.

When someone uses phrases such as, "I don't know" or "I am uncertain," don't rush in with explanations as soon as they say they don't understand something - instead give them space and assess other indicators to gain a fuller picture of their message.

Reading between the lines requires listening closely and considering context, personality and situation when reading a story. An author often does not directly communicate what their characters are trying to express but instead provides situations and clues as to what may be going on for them - the reader can easily recognize this indicator that character is providing.

Here's an excerpt from a story:

Her palms were sweating as she glanced at the clock for the fifth time within an hour, knowing he would arrive around 8. As each second ticked closer and closer towards eight, she could feel her knees weaken and her fists tighten with anticipation of his arrival.

"Honey," asked her husband from across the room. She answered simply. "I am fine; just chilly," was all that was said without making eye contact with him. When her doorbell rang she crouched deeper in her couch with chest tightly hugging knees awaiting an awkward meeting between her husband and his boyfriend.

Did the author indicate that their character was unsettling, yet did you infer this from her body language and the passage? Could you see when she said: "It'll be a long, cold night" that it wasn't just talking about weather? Chances are it happened naturally because an author draws your attention directly to how a character responds in each paragraph of text.

Interacting with real people, however, it's often difficult to pinpoint exactly what's going on even if something seems off. Trust your instincts; even if the source is unclear at first glance. Make a mental note to revisit what was said - for example if one of your siblings or close friends casually mentions being home by six as "Sam gets worried if I am late".

No matter how casual the conversation may seem, something about it feels off. Maybe it was her way of constantly checking time or her rushed tone; or it could simply be words chosen without consideration for context or tone.

"Have to be back home" sounds more like an ultimatum than an expression of concern, which could indicate that she is in an unhealthy relationship with her partner; perhaps neither are aware of the emotional abuse they are experiencing under the name of love and care. Being able to detect what the other person tried to communicate allows us to see beyond what was directly communicated.

Focus on what was unsaid--the silences and pauses--to gain more understanding. Silence may speak volumes; for instance if your child suddenly became silent when asked about their day at school; similarly if words they decided not to speak may indicate problems that are worth paying attention to during other aspects of communication. You could apply this same strategy when engaging with anyone whom you wish to gain a deeper insight.

What questions or topics they avoid discussing; when they pause too long between speaking; does their tone shift when discussing certain people or events; these observations help you understand both them better as individuals as well as comprehending spoken words with greater depth.

Just as when speaking to children about school, when communicating with people who don't readily share information or those who prefer using obscure vocabulary. Your questions and responses must be structured carefully for maximum impact and efficiency.

Make sure you do this all in context; always remain mindful of the situation, setting, and circumstances when observing someone. Be wary if someone sounds distant due to distraction from the environment. Or they might go silent during conversations about certain events - not because they want to conceal anything but instead due to disinterest or distraction from what was being discussed.

Just as understanding someone else requires time, consistency and understanding, so does comprehending what someone says between the lines. Dissecting each word and silence moment by moment would only serve to confuse things further; you need only be present and mindful when listening and mentally review everything you hear before coming up with your conclusions about its possible interpretations.

Chapter 24: Analyzing Speech Patterns

TedTalk audiences don't just witness brilliant ideas presented at TedTalk. Motivators and influencers who succeed aren't necessarily those with great thoughts; they are those who understand how to present them effectively - through tone and pitch practice, categorical structure of speeches or even using media coverage for maximum effect. Public speaking involves mastering how you say things instead of solely considering what needs to be said. Public speakers learn the art of persuasion to win their audiences over.

Public speakers often employ speech patterns to structure their content for maximum effect. The selection of these patterns depends on topics, audiences and the main purpose of their speech - in other words, conversations should serve their true purpose if that's their aim! When speaking with someone new, make sure your goal is clear so you can stay focused when monitoring responses from them - people reading should not involve gathering irrelevant details about others.

Speed Up
A study conducted by the University of Michigan Institute of Social Research examined 1,400 attempts by callers trying to persuade people to participate in a survey, using one phone call per caller per persuasion attempt. [24] Results indicated that those speaking too quickly without pausing were unsuccessful at convincing others; researchers examined callers' fluency, speech rates and pitch when trying to convince others; successful persuaders included people speaking at around 3.5 words per second -- a moderately fast speed when persuading others; [26]

Take the Right Pauses
For maximum influence when trying to influence someone, four or five pauses per minute is ideal when trying to influence someone. These pauses allow the other person to consider your message before responding and show your respect for their thoughts and beliefs while unafraid of allowing their opinions on your findings to develop over time - thus increasing trust between you and them.

Prosody (the stress, intonation of speech and rhythm) is an integral element of effective speech delivery, but too much prosody may backfire and backfire badly. What we say can be perceived differently depending on its delivery - so using tone and rhythm appropriately ensure that what you say gets across exactly as intended; too much may leave an untrusting audience on their hands; try not to sound animated when crafting sentences.

Use Speech Patterns for Success

There are different speech patterns one can employ depending on their goals when speaking publicly, with different choices impacting how successful their message will be delivered. Below are some popular public speaker speech patterns when creating speeches.

Topical or Logical Approach: When conveying multiple ideas that are related, organizing information logically so it flows from topic to topic without appearing like you are jumping between topics without providing convincing arguments is often the best approach.

Chronological: Chronological information organization works best when data needs to follow an orderly progression, such as telling a story. If you want to talk about the outcome of a project, for instance, then structuring events in chronological order for greater clarity will provide greater benefit.

Cause and Effect: As its name implies, this information would be presented using cause-effect relationships. For instance, when discussing issues at work, starting by explaining its cause-then describing how it has an impactful on productivity could serve as the effect.

Problem and Solution: Similar to cause and effect, problem and solution is used as an effective means of persuading others to take actions necessary to solve specific issues. It is an effective method of convincing listeners of how best to approach solving any given challenge or obstacle.

Speech patterns can help communicate ideas and thoughts clearly. People enjoy hearing familiar patterns that they recognize and tend to accept more easily; disoriented information often results in mistrust between parties involved, so investing time into how you deliver your message will increase both credibility and influence over people.

Utilizing an effective speech pattern is key in providing information in an easily digestible fashion and increasing your influence over someone. Your target will view you as an authoritative and logical individual who they can trust more and open up more freely about their ideas and feelings with.

We often form strong connections with someone based solely on how they make us feel. "I don't know why I told you all this; usually I am less open.

What exactly is "vibe", and how can it help me connect to someone? Simply put, vibe is simply good energy that can have a positive influence. No need for giving affirmations or nodding uncontrollably; all it takes to connect is good vibe wherever you go!

Simply ask any motivational speaker or personal development guru and they'd recommend surrounding yourself with positive affirmations about your goals. While it might sound redundant at first, the positive energy soon seeps through and affects us all in one way or another!

That is exactly the effect that positive energy or vibe has on other people. Knowing someone is accepting their ideas without criticism allows them to open up to you without question, giving you access to their mind without questions being raised! All this is made possible when people around them bring positive energy with them - good energy cannot be faked, it can only be detected. Positive attitudes spread quickly - everybody loves talking to people who always see the bright side! And with these tips and strategies for building this positive vibe around you:

Keep Looking on the Bright Side
As they say, your responses to what happens to you determines their outcome. Instead of lamenting over someone being boring to you, use this opportunity to explore ways in which they may think differently than you do and create meaningful interactions. Focusing negatively would only bring out more negativity from you which others would recognize immediately.

If You Don't Feel It, Don't Fake It
Saying you love dogs may come off as hollow; be open-minded enough to accept different viewpoints without forcing agreement onto others; when people realize you accept their right to an opposing viewpoint rather than pretending you like or agree, your response will come across much more positively and welcoming of these differences.

Practice Gratitude
Wondering how gratitude can improve relationships? By beginning and ending each day being thankful for all that life offers us, and honoring those that you encounter on a daily basis such as team leads or siblings by remembering to express appreciation for them every time you interact. Your daily practice of being grateful could even bring positive energy with it when engaging in interactions with them!

Uncover Negativity

Unfortunately, we all can sometimes experience an accumulation of negative thoughts without realizing it. This is particularly the case when we associate certain people with negative memories; for instance if someone made an offensive comment the last time you interacted with them may bring up unpleasant memories that linger long after interaction has ceased. Try replacing negative memories with more upbeat ones in order to create an upbeat environment.

Meditation offers us all an invaluable chance to relax, unwind, and feel grounded. Meditation gives you a wonderful way to release any negative energy around you and evaluate what kind of impact your actions are having on those in your sphere of influence. Furthermore, practicing meditative practices like mindfulness or spirituality could deepen connections to one's inner self and foster deeper peace.

Nature Has Healing Powers
Being outdoors has tremendous healing properties! Surrounded by ocean waves, mountaintop views or riverbank sounds can do wonders for helping us relax and heal from within. Spending time outside has proven itself effective at making people less bitter and more positive - taking a much-needed break while reflecting and taking it easy with ourselves and each other is essential to making sure we remain happy people!
Positive energy in your communications can have a ripple effect on others and encourage them to open up more freely and be honest in their communications with you. Fear of judgements, disappointments or anger could make people close off or lie to avoid appearing unfriendly; providing a comfortable atmosphere and good energy helps people relax so they can reevaluate how they perceive you as well as how much of themselves they're revealing through conversation.

How can one read someone's mind when communicating via carefully constructed emails or phone conversations? Or detect when someone is lying while speaking on the phone? Likewise, how can you interpret between-the-lines communication such as WhatsApp that relies heavily on select "emojis"?

Digital communication offers us many benefits; we can reach people all over the world without leaving our sofas, while at the same time its limitations can limit how effectively we connect. However, with advances in development post-Covid, we have learned how to connect more efficiently. Students were found more attentive in online classes than classroom ones since they couldn't follow their teacher's gaze - without knowing who he/she was watching on their computer screen! However, technology still has some way to go before it can match human warmth and intimacy of one-on-one human contact.

Uncovering someone can be challenging when you don't have their full attention; sleeping, eating or in a crowd. In most instances you won't even be aware if their speaker is on during video calls or reading complete texts before responding - making understanding people across these digital platforms difficult; however there are techniques you can use to accurately interpret what someone is trying to communicate.

Listen I may have mentioned it a number of times already, but firing off criticism and conflict into cyberspace can be easier than communicating directly with someone. While your disagreements might not seem as severe when done over text message, they still limit our ability to listen, read, or understand one another.

Look Out for Indicators

No matter where a person may be located, their tone, choice of words, and environment can all become indicators for how their mind works. For instance, how long is someone taking to respond to emails? Or replying back quickly via text? Or is their voice having any sense of urgency? Paying just a bit of attention can give us invaluable information about them!

Maintain a Calibrated Approach

People can be difficult to read face to face and even more so on screen, which makes misreading their tone, choice of words or pauses even harder. We may misinterpret their text when limited indicators are available to us. Face to face communication allows us to establish an accurate depiction of an individual based on numerous aspects, such as their facial expressions, body language and overall "vibe." As you communicate over the phone or via text with others, make sure that you don't jump to definitive conclusions with limited data. Pay attention to what's being said and ask questions when necessary for clarity. If assumptions arise while conversing, question whether there is enough data available to make accurate observations.

How Can I Spot a Liar Over the Phone or SMS

Lying detection requires keen observational skills; but with many of the usual telltales absent in an SMS text or email conversation, lie detectors provide enough data that allows for accurate detecting over these digital platforms. Here are a few indicators of someone lying to you in writing:

Someone who is telling lies may seem disorganized and difficult to pin down with one storyline, constantly changing subject matters in an attempt to obscure or disguise the truth. They might try overcomplicating things or making up false claims that don't add up; one way of detecting these messages over text messaging could be looking for lengthy paragraphs of text which don't provide clarity about a topic in context; if it were the truth you wouldn't need to read through again to figure out what had really occurred.

They Are Over-emphasizing Unnecessary Information or Avoid Answering Specific Inquiries

If someone asks you a question that requires an answer directly, you could always avoid answering by refusing. Say for instance you asked your partner where they were but received no reply; four hours later they message you to explain that their battery had died but still tell you where they are at that moment - this constitutes lying by omission as they're telling the truth at that time but opt not answer when the inquiry was first made; additionally they may try and provide overly complicated responses as to try and avoid answering directly and derail the conversation altogether.

No One Is Responding

Gone are the days when sending a message was like throwing stones into an ocean without knowing when or if it would reach its recipient; now we know exactly when our message arrived, when it was viewed and whether or not they're "online". Most messaging applications display an ellipsis (...) when someone is typing out their response so we know to expect one any second!

Too Much Information People tend to offer explanations. Ate your co-worker's sandwich at work? Chances are you would offer up an explanation, possibly as long as fifteen minutes long, of why this happened. Similarly when telling lies we tend to use exaggeration in our responses in order to hide what we want people to believe is happening; some individuals regularly create long texts but if responses become unusually lengthy then this could be evidence that they're providing explanations about an information they decided not to reveal.

Imagine being embroiled in a textual argument where both parties are expounding on their respective sides, building lengthy responses until you pose a question and the conversation abruptly shifts away from an answer to another topic. In such an instance, their attempt at being busy could indicate their intent to cut short this conversational thread and move to something else entirely.

"Did You Go To Her House After I Asked You Not to?"

She looked taken aback. It is amazing at how little trust there is between us! Unfortunately I don't have time for this now as there's laundry to be done; talk to you later... Bye."

Here you have it all - all the tools necessary for understanding people. With your guidebook on people in hand, it will enable you to gain an in-depth knowledge of why people speak as they do, behave in certain ways and say what they say - from personality and communication style characteristics through influencers that shape them; all this knowledge is at your fingertips but understanding someone may still require time, effort and a bit of guesswork!

Mind is an intricate structure, and to decipher it one must continue understanding its complexity. Even after knowing someone for years, minor conflicts or disagreements may make it more difficult to listen objectively to what they say.

So I often emphasize the importance of practice and observation when it comes to understanding people. You must exercise control over your own thoughts while showing great adaptability when reading other people's beliefs and styles of communication in order to interpret their words correctly. Here is an outline and reminder of everything you should bring every time you intend to understand someone and untangle the complexities of their unspoken language.

Be Mentally Ready to Read People
Every time you engage in conversation with another, take an inventory of yourself. Ask yourself some key questions such as, * Have I already formed any opinions about them? or >> Are there any biases and prejudices I need to be wary of?

* Am I mentally and emotionally capable of trying to understand someone? * What aspects must be kept in mind when trying to read someone?

*What external factors could possibly sway my judgment? Inquiring this way will enable you to approach others without prejudice or judgment. In order to observe people closely, be attentive - free your mind of other tasks and thoughts so as to focus on observing those of interest without taking them for granted - watch their body language, facial expressions and words closely while listening attentively and without bias.

Spend Time Studying People Mastery of any art takes time and dedication. Reading people requires continual study in order to make accurate assessments about people from diverse backgrounds. In order to do this properly, one needs to observe many individuals from diverse personalities across society in order to form accurate judgments about them. People-reading should be approached holistically. Although it would be nice to understand what your boss thinks or what message your partner is trying to send across the room, to do that properly requires understanding patterns, behaviors and motivations in everyone you come in contact with. For this task, it is necessary to be able to recognize these patterns by observing multiple individuals. Take this skill into consideration when dealing with public commuters or when conversing with salespersons at departmental stores, or even with hairdressers.

Practice makes perfect, as the more often you identify and spot people of various personality types and conversation styles to convey their messages effectively. Furthermore, practicing will allow you to let go of biases and prejudices and observe people without making snap judgments about their character or life situation. People reading skills are an indispensable asset to personal and professional growth, helping you better understand people and their motivations. Recognizing that someone's loudness might not be caused by aggressive speech but by living with an elderly grandparent with hearing loss can give you new perspective. By listening closely when people speak and asking relevant questions about them and showing interest in their stories, it will help you build meaningful relationships both professionally and personally. Spending the time to get to know people will pay dividends both at work and outside it!

Patience and Attentiveness Are Always Necessary
Learning how to knit can be daunting. Practice makes perfect, as do countless attempts at knitting blankets until every knot is perfected - but once the actual task of weaving each knot comes into focus, you become acutely aware of all of the patience, attention, and dedication required in making one swatch of fabric after another. In a similar vein, paying close attention can seem easy in theory, yet sometimes difficult when faced with communicating with those you strongly disagree with or when observing body language of someone you find uninteresting - both tasks take practice if they want results in proper outcomes!

Patience and attentiveness can help you overcome this challenge and gain experience knowing and understanding people from different viewpoints. Only when you patiently listen attentively to someone with whom you disagree will you learn how to observe and read people beyond personal limitations.

Be Authentic and Vulnerable Take mental notes when witnessing someone become distant mid-conversation. People can detect hostility and judgments quickly; they know when someone is trying to walk on eggshells around them. Don't expect someone to open up to you by sitting behind a trench coat with an magnifying glass while trying to be formal or cold towards them; for someone to open up to you they must feel secure enough in opening up themselves freely and safely to you.

Be Open-Minded When Making Your Judgments
This one has been covered often enough, as making quick judgments and assessments about people based on bias and prejudices is the main contributor to them shutting down or you making inappropriate assessments based on them. Practice delaying judgment or conclusions when observing someone. Be wary if your initial thoughts include thinking someone dancing on the street is trying to draw attention - stop yourself there

immediately! For example, if they seem happy enough dancing and you think "they like getting attention", immediately stop yourself before concluding what might be happening - or thinking they just like getting noticed and making assumptions based on assumptions.

Conclusion

At this point, it should be evident that learning to read people is a journey of self-discovery and evaluation; you realize this when realizing it's also about uncovering more about YOU as much as the other person. Doing this helps us recognize limitations within ourselves so we can create deeper and more meaningful connections with one another, ultimately giving us insight into their motivations, aspirations, and most importantly thoughts.

Understand why is the beginning of every journey. No matter if it be business school, medical school or law school--everything starts by first answering this one question--why do things occur as they do. Once this question has been answered, everything else falls into place organically. People-reading is all about answering this question for communication, and once answered it can open up all sorts of possibilities and remove barriers of prejudices and miscommunication. Understanding someone leads to stronger relationships. Skilled communication will serve you throughout life's interactions. From bossing up a team member or convincing parents about your aspirations, to understanding another's motivations and thought trails - knowing your target's motivations gives you leverage to be heard and respected. What an advantage you've found! Each page of this book has been like opening a box full of mysteries related to human behavior - only this book provides only glimpses! Humans don't tend to fall neatly into either black or white categories - they come in all sorts of shades! Chances are, as each day passes you will discover more and more about those living with you. Their reactions could differ depending on life experiences, emotions and environmental influences - to understand them throughout, it's best to stay aware of these changes and adapt accordingly.

So now it is easier than ever to recognize these changes, from bad moods and negative people, to lying and difficulty communicating emotions. Use it wisely and responsibly - the world needs you! Employ these theories at work and with those you value because trees still need the sun's heat and nutrients in good soil for survival. Understanding is necessary in order to be understood, and we need to stay attuned with how people think so we can both protect their interests while understanding our own. May you always use reading wisely as a way of deepening and nurturing meaningful relationships.

THE END

www.ingramcontent.com/pod-product-compliance
Lightning Source LLC
Chambersburg PA
CBHW081351160726
48000CB00010B/3289